STEVE GALLAGHER

OUT OF THE DEPTHS OF SEXUAL SIN

The Story of My Life and Ministry

PURE LIFE MINISTRIES

OUT OF THE DEPTHS OF SEXUAL Sin

ISBN 0-9715470-7-6

For additional copies of this book and
other teaching materials, please contact:

PURE LIFE MINISTRIES
P.O. Box 410
Dry Ridge, KY 41035
888.293.8714
859.824.4444
www.purelifeministries.org

*Note: The names of certain individuals featured in this book
have been changed to protect their privacy.*

Acknowledgements

Special thanks to Robin Little, who put a great deal of effort into this project ten years ago. Also, thanks to Dr. Maureen Haner, Charlie Hungerford, Sharon LaRose, Whitney Long and Pete Nicholson for their important feedback. Thanks also to Bradley Furges who always makes my writing readable.

Dedication

I dedicate this book to the Lord. Everything good in my life has come from His hand. My testimony can be best expressed in the words of David: "This is the God who makes a home for the outcast." (Psalm 68:6)

TABLE OF CONTENTS

Steve Gallagher

INTRODUCTION

y primary purpose for writing this book is to testify to the fact that God can transform the most
wretched life into one of decency. Many struggling believers have been overwhelmed by their shortcom-
ings and sins, feeling as though their problems are insur-
mountable. It would be difficult for anybody to read this book
and walk away feeling as though their problems were beyond God's power to conquer. There is simply no getting away
from the fact that the Lord can and will set the captive free.

However, there is a secondary reason for sharing my
story. It is to refute a widely held notion that change is unimportant in the Kingdom of God. Undoubtedly, everyone
would agree that a Christian should not be held in bondage
to habitual sin, but unfortunately many believe that any
change beyond breaking an addiction is of little conse-
quence—no big deal basically. Their idea is that a person
gets saved, lives a decent life and goes on to heaven some
day. This mentality is grossly unscriptural. From beginning
to end the message of the New Testament is that the Lord
is constantly working in the life of the true believer to mold

him into the image of Christ. Adam Clarke eloquently conveys the importance of progressive sanctification:

> The whole design of God was to restore man to his image, and raise him from the ruins of his fall; in a word, to make him perfect; to blot out all his sins, purify his soul, and fill him with all holiness, so that no unholy temper, evil desire, or impure affection or passion shall either lodge or have any being within him. This and this only is true religion, or Christian perfection; and a less salvation than this would be dishonorable to the sacrifice of Christ and the operation of the Holy Ghost.
>
> We must be made partakers of the divine nature. We must be saved from our sins—from the corruption that is in the world, and be holy within and righteous without, or never see God. For this very purpose Jesus Christ lived, died, and revived, that he might purify us unto himself.[1]

I have done my utmost in this book to be transparent, sharing my deepest struggles and most humiliating failures. Although it was not altogether easy, I have done it knowing that countless others face the same struggles, fears, failures and times of despair as I have faced. If telling about the shameful things I have done and how many times the Lord has bailed me out of trouble will help others see a way out of their troubles, it is well worth it.

My desire is that as you read this story you will be filled with a bright hope that God can bring you out of the depths of whatever you're facing and into a blessed life of joy and freedom just as He has done for me!

---

[1]Ages Software

One

BUSTED!

t was May 1970 and I had just turned sixteen. "Steve, wake up. There's a detective here to see you." It was my dad talking. I looked up through sleepy eyes to see a well-dressed man of about forty, standing there with him. "Did he say detective?" I wondered. Then I noticed what was in his hand and suddenly knew what it was all about. He was holding the three "beautiful" marijuana plants I had been cultivating for some time.

"Hi, Steve, my name is Detective Brown. You're going to have to come with me. Do you mind if I look around your room while you get dressed?"

My mind raced to think of anything else I might have had that was illegal. "No, I don't have anything to hide," I hoped as I nervously watched him search through my stuff.

Every inch of wall was covered with black construction paper. The tin foil in the window made the room pitch black. Checkered over the black paper were psychedelic, black light posters. When the black light was turned on, the room took on a surreal atmosphere. As I tucked my shirt in the detective turned his attention to my bookcase. Sure enough, when he

> *The strife and lack of love in our home created a deep-seated insecurity in me.*

began pulling books out, a joint of marijuana fell out from behind one of them. "Is this yours, Steve?" he asked.

"No," I lied.

After he read me my Miranda rights, we left. I had known it would only be a matter of time before I got busted. There had been so many close calls before. But how providential this arrest would prove to be!

I grew up in a middle class suburb of Sacramento. My dad, who was a supervisor in the civil service, was a very difficult person to live with. He was critical, overbearing, prideful, opinionated and extremely self-centered. He used biting sarcasm to manipulate and control those around him. Jack Gallagher would never admit to being wrong about anything. My mother, sensitive and insecure, simply could not stand up to him. After years of being beaten down emotionally, she eventually closed herself into her own protective shell. The coolness between them made for a miserable marriage, an unhappy home, and an unhealthy environment in which to raise children.

Unfortunately, the strife and lack of love in our home created a deepseated insecurity in me. Although my mother tried to maintain discipline with my older half-sister and me, my dad was erratic and inconsistent in how he dealt with us. You never knew what to expect from him. Rather than discipline me out of love, he always tried to force me to do what he wanted me to do in anger. His idea of love was to spoil me by letting me have my way—as long as it didn't bother him—and to buy me things.

One incident when I was about 12 years old typifies

what it was like living with him. My sister Kathy was from my mom's first marriage, and my dad never let her forget that she wasn't his child. We were eating dinner, and he began criticizing her over something petty. In an attempt to defend her, I blurted out, "Why don't you get off her back?"

As soon as the words left my mouth, he backhanded me right out of my chair. I stormed into my bedroom and shed tears of humiliation into my pillow. Shortly thereafter, he came into the room and attempted to make up for what he'd done. But I was determined that it wasn't going to work this time and ignored him for several days. Eventually he tried to make amends with me. He knew that I really wanted a certain locomotive for my train set. "Look, Steve, if you quit pouting, I'll buy you that locomotive you want." Swallowing my pride was acceptable if it meant getting something I really wanted. I reluctantly agreed.

One of the few things that I didn't get my way with was going to church. I was forced to attend services at the large Southern Baptist church my mother belonged to.* Sometimes I would cut Sunday school, take the fifty cents my mom gave me for the offering, and go spend it in a nearby doughnut shop. Nevertheless, in spite of my poor attitude, the pastor's sermons were getting through, and one Sunday morning I responded to an altar call. "There was no stopping Steve from going forward that morning," my mother later said. Unfortunately, little seemed to change in my life afterwards.

---

* My mother (Frances) had been a Christian since childhood. Her close relationship to the Lord helped her endure her life with my father. Many nights I would come home in the early morning hours high on drugs to find her sitting in her favorite rocking chair with her Bible sitting open on her lap. For the next 30 years she faithfully ministered to children as a Sunday school teacher, finally retiring from this service in her late seventies. She is 80-years-old, as of the writing of this book, and her faith in God remains as robust as ever.

Although I was a selfish, mouthy, spoiled brat, I really didn't start getting into trouble until the sixth grade. I began to hang around with two rabble-rousers who were feared and respected by the other kids because they were such troublemakers. Being their friend brought me the same notoriety.

Our mischief wasn't anything too serious at first: throwing eggs at houses, picking on other kids, shooting spit wads at the teacher when her back was turned, and so on. As we entered junior high school, the trouble gradually became more serious. We began to experiment with drugs. It started with sniffing glue, but before long we were excitedly smoking our first "joint" of marijuana.

It was also about this time that a cousin from Ohio came to live with us. One day, I stumbled upon one of his *Playboy* magazines and scanned its pages from cover to cover with wide-eyed astonishment. Over the next two years, I returned to his secret cache of magazines again and again. It was during one of these forays that I discovered masturbation, which quickly developed into a regular routine.

During junior high school I made a number of clumsy attempts at seducing girls but didn't "go all the way" with a girl until age fifteen. She became my girlfriend for a short time—until I grew bored with her and began looking for another lover. This established a pattern of developing short-term relationships with girls. Each new cutie would fascinate me at first. Everything about the girl's physique would inflame my lust. She became the sole recipient of all my self-serving desires. She would bask in all of this attention, convinced that she was my one and only. However, once we went to bed together, I began looking for my next prey.

There were two powerful passions that drove me to seduce girls. One was simply an insatiable desire for variety. If my current girlfriend was a blond, I would become fascinated with brunettes or red-heads—or perhaps a girl of a different race. The female figure—tall, petite, buxom, or slender—also enthralled me. The possibilities were endless.

> *Another contributing factor to my internal misery was an unrelenting, tormenting fear of others.*

The other motivating factor involved was the need to improve my image to those around me. Every young lady "conquered" became another "notch on my belt." Every conquest enhanced my reputation as being a "ladies man."

By the ninth grade our gang was totally immersed in the drug culture. It was 1969 and we absorbed the rebellious music of the Doors, Janis Joplin, Led Zeppelin and Jimi Hendrix. We idolized the Hell's Angels, who occasionally roared up to parties we attended on their Harley Davidsons. We all longed for the day we could afford to buy our own "choppers."

Those early days of smoking marijuana were enormously exciting. I got high just about every day throughout the ninth and tenth grades. However, over time smoking dope became almost drudgery—not much better than the excruciating boredom of being sober. Never afraid of trying something new, I started injecting drugs. Once I experienced the rush of barbiturates (reds) and methamphetamine (speed) through my body, nothing else would do. Eventually this escalated to shooting up opium and heroin. It got so bad that, wanting others to see me as being fearless, I would recklessly shoot up large quantities of drugs at a time. I was miserable inside and simply didn't care if I lived or died.

Another contributing factor to my internal misery was an unrelenting, tormenting fear of others. My deep-seated

Despite all my brashness and "tough guy" façade, I was also very sensitive.

anxiety about people advanced until I was constantly bombarded with paranoid thoughts. My daily dosage of hallucinogenic drugs (i.e. marijuana, LSD, mescaline, and peyote) magnified this unreasonable fear. Although many hallucinogenic trips turned into bad experiences, I continued to self-medicate.

My difficult, abrasive personality resulted in strained relations with others. Having an intense, excitable and angry character tended to alienate me from other people. My harsh and unbearable nature usually invoked fear or outright anger in most people. No matter how hard I tried to be different, my words always carried a certain undertone of sarcasm or hostility.

Despite all my brashness and "tough guy" façade, I was also very sensitive. I can remember, as a child, feeling terribly vulnerable and fearful of the cutting remarks of my classmates, the abrasive comments of my father, and the foolish jokes of my friends. Underneath my tough exterior was a thin suit of skin.

In the meantime, the fear of being seen as a "chump" grew within me. I did my best to keep up with the others, but some of my acquaintances were vicious. The drugs continued to take their toll on my confidence level.

One particular night the fear simply took over my mind. I went to a Hell's Angels' party with a friend. It wasn't easy for me as a fifteen-year-old to maintain my image around these hardened bikers. We were all sitting around the living room passing around one "reefer" after another. I made the foolish mistake of taking a tab of acid and gradually began to lose touch with reality. The sense of everybody being against me grew in my mind. The more fixated I became on this thought the more I panicked inside. Frantically, I tried to think of a way to get out of there without drawing attention to myself. Not knowing what to do, I finally laid down right there on the living room floor and acted like I had passed out. It was the only way to get out of the situation and still maintain my "cool."

Actually I was wide awake all night long and was convinced that everyone there had been talking about me. The reality, of course, was that nobody was paying much attention to this kid in their midst. Nevertheless, from that night on, fear plagued my life. No matter how confident I tried to appear, I was terrified that my friends would see me as a "chump"—someone to be taken advantage of.

***

The summer of 1969 was a wild one. By this point I had begun to develop friendships with an older and more hardened crowd. During the week—while my parents were at work—my house was a hangout spot for various drug users. On the weekends, we would have wild parties at various locations.

One huge party was the Amador Pop Festival. Thousands of people attended this massive drug-fest. We arrived there around noon. Music was being played on a stage in a small valley, and people were seated or laying all of the way up the hillside. I took some LSD and was once again gripped with overwhelming fear. To counter the effects of the "acid," I sat down in the middle of the crowd and shot up some barbiturates.

I stumbled through the crowd—sometimes stepping on irritated people—and finally ended up in the Hell's Angels' camp. They had thrown a tractor tire into the campfire caus-

Memories of giving my life to Jesus in that Baptist church years earlier were far from my mind.

ing black smoke to billow up into the atmosphere. One of the HA's (as we admiringly called them) had a whip attached to a wrist-band and was snapping any hapless person who walked by. Every time he would thrash someone he would let out a hideous bellow of laughter. The others would join in the fun, too. Before long, the inevitable gallon of cheap wine—made milky by dumping dozens of "reds" into it—made its way around the circle. I dutifully gulped some, passed it on to the next guy and stumbled off into the crowd looking for my friends.

Parties weren't our only source of entertainment. We regularly drove around at night smoking marijuana and drinking beer or wine. One day a few of us went for a drunken ride in a car owned by the mother of one of the guys. As we recklessly rode around, the guy behind the driver put his hands over his eyes, while the rest of us laughed. We were speeding down backcountry roads, whooping it up. As we zipped around a curve, suddenly the asphalt ended and the road became gravel. In a panic, the driver slammed on the brakes. The car fishtailed into a ditch and rolled over twice. When someone yelled that it was going to blow up, we all scrambled out to safety. Once we realized none of us were badly hurt, we all got a big laugh out of it—that is, everyone except for the guy who had to go tell his mother we had totaled her uninsured car.

Recklessness constituted my daily life. Memories of giving my life to Jesus in that Baptist church years earlier were far from my mind. Little did I know then that God had His hand on me and was sparing my life for a reason. Twelve of my friends were killed during this period of my life, but this didn't bother me very much. Being extremely selfish, my only concern about someone dying was how it might affect me personally. For the most part, a friend getting killed only tended to reinforce my image of being tough and fearless.

Summer was soon over, and it was time to start high school. My friends and I would often skip classes to smoke pot. During the first six months of the school year, I was suspended six different times for cutting school, stealing or smoking. The seventh time I asked the vice principal to expel me, which he did without hesitation.

I was transferred to a "continuation school" for troublesome students. It only had two classrooms and two teachers. They tried to keep some semblance of order, but it was simply impossible. We would actually smoke weed in the classroom some days. I even had marijuana plants growing in the teacher's flower-box.

My friend Randy and I quickly became the ringleaders. At least that's what our teacher told the detectives who arrived one day to investigate the theft of her purse. That evening, the investigators came to my house and told me that Randy had already admitted that we had taken it. (This was a favorite trick of cops to get people to confess their crimes.) This ploy didn't work simply because we really hadn't taken it. They told me to retrieve the wallet and everything would be forgotten. "She doesn't care about the money, she just wants her credit cards back," the big one said.

"I'll see what I can do," I muttered. I asked around and discovered that a guy named Ray had taken the purse. He gave the wallet to me and—after taking the money out for my trouble—I gave it back to the teacher.

Ray and I had another run-in a few weeks later when he ripped off a friend of mine for a thousand reds. He asked a tough black guy for protection, promising him part of the

> *The more miserable and fearful I became, the more I turned to drugs in an attempt to escape reality.*

stash for his efforts. That made us mad. I knew his "bodyguard," so after squaring things with him, we went after Ray. I treacherously tricked him into walking into a field with me, where my three friends were waiting. We were walking along having a conversation when I suddenly turned and slugged him in the stomach. My friends quickly appeared, and one of them blindsided him with a punch to the head. Each of us hit him a couple of times, but we were too loaded on barbiturates to hurt him very much. Unbeknownst to me, Ray would soon lead me to the biggest score of my life.

The more miserable and fearful I became, the more I turned to drugs in an attempt to escape reality. To get money for dope, I began dealing drugs and burglarizing homes. My world was becoming darker and darker. Everything left me miserable, hopeless and empty inside.

One night Randy and I broke into a house and ransacked it from one end to the other. The people pulled up in the driveway while we were in the house. We both ran to the backdoor. Not only was the doorknob locked, but it had a chain lock on it as well. We were in such a frenzy to get out that every time I tried to unlock the chain, he would yank the door, tightening the chain. As the people came in the front door, Randy pulled the door so hard that the chain ripped out of the wall. We ran through the backyard and started jumping fences to get away.

On another occasion we stole a television set. We put it in the trunk of my car to take it to a heroin dealer's house, but it was too big to close the trunk-lid. Driving all the way across Sacramento in the middle of the night with a stolen

TV hanging out of the back of the car was absolutely absurd, but we were desperate. We traded it for a little balloon filled with heroin and headed home.

We had almost made it home when a sheriff's patrol car pulled us over. Randy put the balloon in his mouth just as the officer approached the car.

"Would you mind getting out, please?"

"Sure, officer," I confidently responded. "What's the problem?"

"No problem, just put your hands on the hood. Let's see what you have in your pockets."

It was a routine "roust." The cops searched us both. As one questioned me, the other began hunting for drugs in the car. I chattered nervously while Randy remained quiet. When they came to the conclusion that we didn't have anything, they released us. Randy pulled the balloon out of his mouth, and we began laughing out of relief. We quickly drove to my house and shot up our bag of "H."

Randy went home at dawn and I fell into a deep sleep, not waking up until my parents returned home from work. I must have looked pretty disgusting to them. My thick, brown hair was hanging around my shoulders, and my jeans were filthy and ragged. After all, the Hell's Angels never washed theirs!

I took a shower and joined them for dinner. I quickly ate my food, wanting to get back out to the streets where the action was. I could hardly endure being in the presence of "straight" people. They didn't understand anything. My parents didn't approve of my lifestyle but never reached out in warmth and love. My problems were too overwhelming to my mother, and my father simply didn't care.

As we ate in silence, my dad told me that he wanted me to quit hanging around with my friends. "Why?" I asked—

not that I had the slightest intention of obeying him.

"Because they're a bad influence on you," he responded.

It was clear that he didn't have a proper understanding of the situation. "Dad, I'm the one that's a bad influence on them!" I informed him.

———

It was a warm June morning in 1970. My father stayed home from work that day so he could take me to court. I stood before the juvenile judge full of contempt and rebellion. I had been charged with one felony count of cultivation of marijuana and a misdemeanor count of possession of marijuana. The judge sentenced me to twenty days of Work Project and told me to report to the juvenile detention center at 7:30 a.m. the following Monday.

Work Project was a program that required youth offenders to do manual labor for the state. I only recognized two faces out of the group of teenagers who stood waiting there Monday morning. One was Ray and the other was the black guy he had hired to protect him in the barbiturate deal. Before long a work officer arrived with a bus, and we all boarded to go off to our work assignment for the day.

It was hard work in the middle of a hot, California summer, and the next month seemed to last forever. Somehow I showed up for work everyday and tried to stay out of trouble. Arriving home at night too tired to party, I remained fairly straight that month.

As those four weeks went by, an inexplicable phenomenon began to occur within me as the drug haze wore off. Although

> *I was living a completely degenerative life, and yet began to control my words. I had no idea that it was the conviction of the Holy Spirit.*

thoughts of God or Christianity never entered my mind, I started to feel a sense of guilt anytime I took the Lord's name in vain. I was living a completely degenerative life, and yet began to control my words. I had no idea that it was the conviction of the Holy Spirit.

Finally my last day of Work Project arrived. I already had a date lined up that night with a girl I had just met. She would be the focus of my celebration that evening.

I arrived at the job site that morning to find that our work for the day was to be comparatively easy. All we had to do was to clear the weeds out of a street center divider. I was working by myself raking leaves when Ray approached me. "You'll never guess what happened to me last night," he said abruptly.

"What?" I asked, with a lack of interest.

"I got born again," he replied.

"What do ya' mean, ya' got born again?"

"I turned my life over to God."

"Whaddja' do that for?" Could this be the same Ray who had always been in so much trouble?

"Steve, I found out that you gotta' give your heart to Jesus or you'll go to hell."

"Oh, is that what you're talkin' about? I went up to the altar when I was a kid and got baptized the next week. I'm already covered," I said confidently.

Ray told me that being baptized is not the same as being born again. "When a person is truly born again his life changes," he explained.

"When did all this happen?" I asked with piqued interest.

Ray told me what had happened to him the night before. He had been walking around the local mall when he heard something going on behind it. Walking around to the back to check it out, he discovered that some people were hold-ing a revival service. Ray sat in a chair in the back—ready to make a quick get-away if he had to. As the evangelist began preaching, he felt as though he were speaking right to him. When the altar call was given, he practically ran to the front. "All I can tell you," he said, summing up his story, "is that I have never felt so good in all my life!"

As Ray talked, something began stirring within me. His testimony didn't make much sense, but a conviction was welling up inside me that I had to have what he was describ-ing.

"They're havin' meetings all week if you wanna' go," he exclaimed.

"I gotta' date tonight, but I'll go tomorrow night," I prom-ised.

I had a miserable evening as the thought that I could be killed and go to hell loomed over me like an ominous cloud before a thunderstorm. Honestly, I couldn't wait to go to that meeting.

Two

JESUS FREAK

The revival meeting was set up behind the bowling alley located near the mall. The only props were a small wooden stage, a big sign over it reading "Jesus Festival," and about two hundred folding chairs. Standing on the makeshift platform was a band of longhaired young people tuning their guitars and occasionally letting loose with brief flurries of loud music.

Ray and I took a seat and watched the cheerful activity going on around us. I felt completely out of place. Still a full-fledged member of Satan's kingdom, I suspiciously eyed those around me. They seemed to be genuinely warm and open with each other and were far different from the mean-spirited hoodlums who populated my little world. They possessed a certain joy that seemed unattainable. Full of darkness, I sat in my chair, terribly lost and bound for hell.

Eventually the band started to play. This was not like the rock concerts I had attended. Everybody stood up and began exuberantly singing along with them! Their music had a purity about it that was poles apart from the evil lyrics that had previously saturated my mind.

> *I didn't need a lot of coaching. For the first time in my life, I felt as though there was hope.*

After singing several songs, the people sat down and the evangelist, Ron Stillwell, came up to the podium. My perspective of Christianity had been warped by years of rebellion and sin. I assumed that he would deliver an angry fire-and-brimstone sermon. Instead, Ron quietly began talking about what it feels like to be lost. He described in intimate detail the very sense of hopelessness that was my daily portion. He only spoke for about half an hour before he brought his message to a close.

"Maybe some of you here tonight feel like you have nothing to live for," he said. "You've tried all kinds of things in life but nothing satisfies. I want to tell you that Jesus Christ can set you free and give you a new life." Pointing to the small area in front of the stage he continued, "If you want to receive eternal life tonight, I want you to meet me down here right now."

I didn't need a lot of coaching. For the first time in my life, I felt as though there was hope. Ray leaned over to me and whispered, "Steve, I'll go down there with you if you want to go."

"Okay, let's go," I replied. With that simple statement, I made my first step toward Christ.

From that night on Ray and I became inseparable in our new life of Christianity. Sundays and Wednesday nights were spent in church. On weekends, a group of us would show up at the mall to hand out evangelistic tracts to passersby.

We felt like we had been given the key to a bottomless gold mine and were told to give away as much of it as we could. We were amazed that everybody we approached didn't immediately drop to his or her knees in repentance. Some did, though.

On one occasion, we all piled into our cars and drove to a hippie hangout. We went inside to share Christ with people, but they weren't interested. Discouraged, we went outside, sat on the grass and began praying. One of the guys started asking the Lord to send someone out to talk to us. Sure enough, a few minutes later a young guy came out and asked us what we were doing. We explained that we were Christians and told him about the Lord. He accepted the Lord right then and there. A little while later someone asked him why he had come outside. He said that he had been painting in a room upstairs when he started getting an unshakeable sense that he should go outside.

This kind of experience wasn't altogether foreign to us in those days. We were excited about God, and our simple faith allowed us to believe for great things from Him. We didn't know it at the time, but we were part of a move of God among the troubled youth of the day that would become known as the "Jesus Movement." People laughingly called us "Jesus Freaks."

Another contributor to my budding faith was reading biographies of great Christian leaders. I was fascinated by the modern-day stories of Brother Andrew and David Wilkerson and the great missionaries of old such as Jonathan Goforth, William Carey, Hudson Taylor and David Livingstone. Their accounts of living by faith, witnessing God's miraculous power, and being used by Him to bring souls into the Kingdom thrilled me. These testimonies of men of faith compelled me to press on as a believer. And yet, something deeper was happening in my heart: *God was calling me into His service.*

I spent countless hours fantasizing about being in the ministry. I was torn between wanting to be a missionary and an evangelist. Reading the stories about missionaries living by faith incited a desire within me to run a ministry that had to trust God for its survival from month to month. However, when I attended the services of visiting evangelists, I would dream of being such a preacher myself. I knew God had His mighty hand on my life, but the reality of actually being a minister seemed far-fetched.

Meanwhile, Ray and I began going around to all of our old haunts to witness to our former friends. We excitedly told them about what the Lord had done in our lives. We were confident they would want what we had if they could only be made to understand it. They were amazed to see the change in us. We cut our hair and replaced our dirty, ratty jeans with clean ones.

One night I ran into Randy. He had already heard about what had happened in my life and was somewhat curious about what I had to say. When I told him about my salvation experience, how a wave of joy had overwhelmed me, and how I felt like a thousand pounds had come off my back, he agreed to do it himself. He bowed his head and repeated the sinner's prayer. "I don't feel no different," he stated flatly. As we talked, it became obvious to me that he wasn't interested in surrendering his life to God, he was just trying out a new experience in the same way he might try some new drug. It was a great disappointment to see nearly all my former friends reject the gospel.

Ray and I were like relentless salesmen, though. We kept showing up at hangouts and parties, hoping for the opportunity to lead someone to the Lord. One night, we were arrested at a party that was raided and had to spend the night in juvenile hall. We later explained to our probation officer what had happened, and he got the charges dropped. Our clean-cut appearance and constant talk of Jesus made it obvious to him that we had really changed.

Our efforts to share Jesus with our old friends were mostly unsuccessful. Before long, the novelty of the Jesus Freaks faded, and people would scatter when

What began with so much bright hope ended in futility and discouragement.

they saw us coming. They grew tired of us badgering them. Like so many new converts, we had far more zeal than wisdom.

As the months rolled by, my newfound enthusiasm began to wane as well. I had been attempting to maintain Christianity by emotionally pumping myself up. There seemed to be a certain kind of strength from the excitement of seeing miracles, hearing leading evangelists, and watching end time prophecies unfold. However, I lacked the proper foundation of the Christian faith that comes from being connected to God through the disciplines of daily prayer and Bible study. I desperately needed a mentor who would take an interest in me and disciple me.

Another nagging problem that never seemed to lose its power was masturbation. Nobody had to tell me it was wrong because anytime I gave in to those urges a heavy sense of conviction came upon me. Giving up my new girlfriend hadn't been too difficult, but this problem seemed impossible to conquer. The disappointment of repeated failures eventually brought me to the place where I quit fighting altogether. I was weary of feeling like a hypocrite and finally backslid after nine months of Christianity. What began with so much bright hope ended in futility and discouragement.

My old friends had a great time of laughing at me once I returned to the fold. "We knew it would only be a

Weeks rolled into months as the happy memories of Christianity seemed to fade into oblivion. matter of time, Steve!" they said. I tried to explain to them that I still believed in Christ, but those words sounded pretty weak coming from someone with a joint in his mouth.

Although I went back to my old lifestyle, I *was* different inside. The deep sense of hopelessness that had controlled me to the point of having a death wish was no longer there. "Even if I can't seem to serve God now, one day I will," I would tell myself. However, as I began to smoke dope again, the old feelings of fear returned in full force. What made it worse now was that by becoming a Christian I had shown weakness. Weeks rolled into months as the happy memories of Christianity seemed to fade into oblivion.

One night, I was sitting in my car in front of my house smoking a joint with a friend. The fear had caused me to become cautious about where I went. Suddenly, my old friend Randy, his older brother Jim, a Hispanic guy named Johnny, and a black guy named Roy showed up. I knew all these guys well. Randy had been my best friend. Jim had been to prison and was known for his ruthlessness. Johnny made up for his small stature with an explosive temper. Roy was an old friend I had partied with many times in the past.

As soon as they walked up, I could smell trouble. They were high on reds and alcohol and were bragging about how they had just "rat-packed" and "stomped into the ground" some hapless victim. "We messed him up!" Randy exclaimed. I was trying to be my old self, laughing along with them, but they saw right through it.

My companion left immediately. They all climbed into the car as Jim insisted I find them some girls. I drove around aimlessly, trying to figure out how to get rid of them. They acted like rabid, fighting dogs, laughing one minute and yelling at each other the next. Before long their ugliness was directed toward me.

With a menacing voice, Jim told me to pull the car over. I felt helpless to stand up against his hatred. I dutifully pulled over, and we all got out of the car. Johnny accused me of stealing his girlfriend a couple of years prior to this. I tried to protest, but what he said was true. Apparently he had been bitter over this incident this whole time.

The four of them circled me threateningly. I looked to Randy, hoping to see pity on his face but found none. Johnny started talking about the different ways he was going to hurt me. Jim kept provoking him, telling him to hit me. They could "smell blood" and were waiting for an excuse to attack me themselves. I tried to reason with Johnny, sensing that he really didn't want to fight me. He seemed to be putting on a show for Jim, who was my real antagonist. Suddenly Roy stepped between us to defend me and temporarily defused the situation. Finally, we all got back into the car.

As I drove, Jim put his hands over my eyes from behind so I couldn't see where I was going. He then erupted into the evilest laugh I had ever heard. It was obvious he was possessed by a devil. I pretended to drive aimlessly, but I made my way back to my house. I pulled along the curb and mumbled something about going in to call some girls. As I scampered to the front door, I heard Jim yell, "Get the knife. He's gonna' call the cops!" I made it to the front door, but I was shaking so badly that I couldn't get the key into the lock. Just as they were coming up behind me, I finally unlocked the door and darted inside.

This experience devastated me. I went into a depression that lasted for months, refusing to go outside or to see any-

Unable to live the Christian life, and yet, unhappy as a sinner, it seemed as though there was nowhere to turn.

one. I was convinced that my friends had labeled me the lowest coward that ever lived. In reality, it was probably no big deal to anybody, but I was so consumed with what people thought of me that it crushed me. I was in a prison of self once again.

This was one of the lowest points of my entire life. Unable to live the Christian life, and yet, unhappy as a sinner, it seemed as though there was nowhere to turn. People didn't like me and I didn't like them. It seemed as though I had become insane. I was obsessed with the thought that everyone around me—whether it was my family, friends or people out in public that didn't even know me—saw me as a worthless, no-good person.

One day, I apprehensively drove to K-Mart. As I walked down one of the aisles, a young teenage girl laughingly shoved her friend into me. Convinced they thought I was weird, I made a mad dash for home and sequestered myself back into the safety of my home. I didn't understand at the time that my paranoia came from being so prideful and consumed with myself.

For several months I escaped reality by watching television for hours on end everyday. The good thing that came out of this incident was the realization that I would never again fit in with the biker crowd. Although I would occasionally dabble with drugs after that, they never again ruled my life.

As time went on and my thinking became clearer, my confidence grew. Eventually, I took a high school equivalency test and enrolled in a junior college. Seducing girls became my main purpose in life. I targeted those that seemed needy for affection. Each time my routine remained essentially the same. I would meet a girl, treat her like she was the most important person on earth, convince her to have sex, and then dump her.

I met my match in a girl named Stephanie. She was a tiny, cute-faced girl with long black hair. In spite of the fact that she was a virgin—and planned to stay that way—I kept working on her until she "fell in love" with me and allowed me to have my way. Her virginity made her special to me, and we became inseparable.

One evening, we were at a friend's house drinking and taking reds (barbiturates) which are known for making people combative. Stephanie and I got into an ugly argument. It started over some trivial thing, but it escalated as we both continued to provoke each other. Finally, in exasperation, I told her to shut up or she was going to leave.

"I'm not leaving and you can't make me leave," she yelled. Too proud to respond with the gentleness that quells arguments (Proverbs 15:1), I attempted to end the argument by grabbing her and dragging her to the door. She began screaming hysterically. I slapped her, thinking it would calm her down. Unfortunately, the adrenaline flowing through me caused me to hit her harder than I intended. She flew back and hit her head on the wall. It knocked her out.

She didn't come to consciousness until the next day. I apologized and everything seemed to be okay. However, after she had been up for awhile, she passed out again. We put her into my car and raced her to the hospital. "She's not breathing, and I can't feel a pulse!" my friend yelled, as we pulled into the emergency entrance. Not knowing if she was alive or not, I ran into the waiting room and told the male receptionist that I thought the girl in my car was dying. He calmly asked my name, address and so on. When I screamed at him to do something, he jumped out of his chair and got her into the emergency room. They resuscitated her, but she had several more relapses during the following week.

Her parents wouldn't let me see her or tell me how she was. During this whole time I was in a daze, not knowing if she would live or die. It didn't help when two detectives visited one day, asking me to make a statement. It was clear that prison was a real possibility. For several days, I pleaded with God to save her life. She recovered, and eventually I returned to my old lifestyle of chasing girls.

A couple of months later, I ran into Stephanie at a local store. We started seeing each other again, and when her dad found out about it, he gave me the ultimatum to either marry her or quit seeing her. At 20 years of age, I really didn't want to get married but couldn't bear the idea of not seeing her again. We had a small wedding on December 14, 1974.

Having a wife changed the direction of my life. The carefree college life was gone. I learned how to run a printing press and spent the next few years in the field of graphic arts. We eventually bought a small house in a run-down area of town.

One day, we visited my parents. My dad was drunk—which occurred frequently. Stepping out for a few minutes, I returned to find Stephanie in tears. I took her into the bathroom and asked her what was wrong. She was reluctant to tell me why she was upset. Finally, she acknowledged that my dad had inappropriately touched her breast.

Years of anger and resentment welled up inside me. In a rage, I rushed into the living room where he was standing and hit him so hard his feet came off the ground. He was out cold before he hit the floor. We gathered our things and went out to the car. By this time he had returned to consciousness and had gotten his revolver. He aimed it at me, but we left before he could fire a shot.

As I immersed myself in this dark, seedy world, perspectives changed, inhibitions fell away and shame dissolved.

Stephanie and I stayed together for two and a half years, but it was never meant to be. I was mean and domineering, just like my father had been with my mother. Worst of all, I committed adultery with other young women several times. In 1977, she finally left me and filed for divorce.

Feeling as though printing was a dead-end career, I eventually decided to go into real estate sales. I made a number of sales during my first month, launching what seemed to be a successful career. To enhance my image of success, I bought a luxury car.

Also during this time I discovered adult bookstores. I was so ashamed the first time I visited one I looked around to make sure nobody saw me enter before I darted in the door. I was absolutely enthralled with what I discovered there. The walls of the store were lined with explicit magazines, and there were also private booths where one could watch X-rated films. There were only a couple of other men in the store and I flushed with a combination of embarrassment and excitement. From that day on, I became intoxicated with hard-core pornography. I continued dating, but my new pastime saved me the hassle of pursuing relationships.

I also discovered strip clubs, street prostitutes and massage parlors at this time. A whole new world had opened up to me. I continued dating girls whenever possible, but primarily my sex life involved secret sexual excursions that didn't involve relationships. As I immersed myself in this dark, seedy world, perspectives changed, inhibitions fell away and shame dissolved. For a short period of time, I was actually fairly happy. I did not realize the tremendous price sin would eventually exact upon my life. At the time, I could only see the immediate gratification.

Three

A LITTLE BLOND AND THE L.A.S.D.

*L*ife seemed so promising as 1979 unfolded. My new career in real estate began to take off. I drove a nice car and finally felt as though I had something worthwhile to live for. I even began to entertain the thought of finding a Christian wife and getting right with God again.

One day in January I ran into an old friend named Keith. He had spent time in prison for killing a couple of people (including Randy—the guy who had played such a large part of my early life). I hadn't seen him in years. Since he had been released from prison, Keith had gotten married and had two children. When he heard that I was selling real estate, he invited me to his home. "I'm coming into some money, Steve, and I'd like to buy a house."

A few days later I went to see him—not desiring to reestablish a relationship but simply hoping to sell a house. I pulled into his driveway and was disappointed to see that his home was nothing more than a shack. Keith answered the door with a welcoming smile. "Come on in, Steve," he said, motioning me to enter his home.

And then I saw her—like a rose blooming in the middle of a dung heap—a pretty, little blond.

Before my eyes even adjusted to the dark, I knew the place was filthy. An overpowering odor of unchanged diapers and stale marijuana smoke hung in the air. As my eyes became accustomed to the dark surroundings, I took in the scene that was before me. Keith's overweight wife Paula sat on the couch, with a child on either side of her. Children's clothing and toys were strewn all around the living room. I could see into the kitchen behind her, where a stack of unwashed dishes teetered next to the sink. And then I saw her—like a rose blooming in the middle of a dung heap—a pretty, little blond warming her back on the wall heater.

I tried to act nonchalant about her, but it was all I could do to exchange greetings with Paula. After what seemed like an eternity, Keith turned toward the petite young girl and said, "This is my brother's wife, Kathy." My heart sank, but I managed to say hello.

After spending some time reminiscing about the "good ole' days," Keith began to explain his desire to buy a house. I tried to pay attention, but my eyes kept involuntarily moving toward the heater. It soon became quite obvious that he really wasn't a serious buyer.

After awhile, Keith and I went out to the front yard. He could see my obvious interest in Kathy and, to my great relief, told me that she had separated from his brother and had filed for divorce. He lit up a joint, which I politely declined to share with him, and began to tell me about Kathy.

She had grown up in North Sacramento, a depressed part of town with an abundance of crime and drugs. Kathy had attended a tough high school, where Afro-Americans and Hispanics outnumbered Caucasians. Her blond hair made her stand out all the more. Although she had an easy-going nature, she was harassed regularly by a group of Mexican girls who intensely disliked her and continually attempted to pick fights with her. One time, during gym class, they jimmied open her locker and threw all her clothes into the showers. Another time they broke into her house and ransacked her bedroom. Nearly every day after school these girls would taunt her and push her around.

Kathy's home had an interesting mixture of love and strife. Her parents, Mel and Shirley Irwin, truly loved each other and their five kids. However, Mel's occasional bouts of drinking made him belligerent and unreasonable. Even though Kathy loved her family, she was desperate to get out of her house.

When she was sixteen, she met David, Keith's younger brother. He was a biker who longed to join the Hell's Angels. Two weeks after the two met, they got married in Reno and immediately moved into a dumpy apartment to begin their new life together. It didn't take Kathy long to find out that this marriage was not going to be like that of her parents. In true biker fashion, David treated his young wife as if she were subhuman. Whenever the gang would go to their favorite bar, the "ole ladies" were expected to sit outside on the motorcycles. Kathy had a natural modesty that helped her tolerate this degrading treatment. What she couldn't put up with were the beatings she received from David over every petty disagreement. He thought nothing of kicking her or hitting her right in the mouth.

One day, he beat her so badly that she had to be admitted into the hospital. She was hemorrhaging and found out later that she had a miscarriage. At this point she decided that she had had enough. She left him and filed for divorce.

Since David never went to his brother's house, Kathy continued her friendship with Paula and would often visit them.

There was something about her that attracted me the minute I saw her. Her winsome personality made her appear as if she didn't have a care in the world. Her bright smile seemed to infect everyone around her. Even all the physical and mental abuse she had experienced couldn't dampen her zest for life.

I began frequenting Keith's house in the hopes of running into Kathy. Although I seized every opportunity to strike up conversations with her, she remained aloof. After what she had been through with David, she was not interested in getting involved with another man. However, to my surprise and delight, Keith and Paula seemed anxious to see us together.

With their encouragement—and my insistence—she finally agreed to go out on a date with me. We went out a couple more times after that, but she kept her distance. Finally, in a bold move, I asked her to spend a weekend with me in Santa Cruz, a beachside resort. Kathy later related what happened:

> One day, after we had been dating for a while, Steve asked me to go to Santa Cruz with him for the weekend. I needed to clarify if that meant we would be in the same motel room together because in my thinking that would mean a commitment on my part to give myself to him. It meant I would have to drop my guard and give my heart as well. He told me that yes we would be staying together.

Santa Cruz is where I decided I wanted to spend the rest of my life with Steve Gallagher.

It was one of the biggest decisions of my adult life. In my mind, it was the same as marrying him because, if I gave myself to him, it meant that I was his and he was mine. This wasn't just a date or a fun weekend with some guy I liked. I had never done anything like this before. Yet, in some way, I felt as though I was being pulled helplessly into this relationship and I couldn't fight it. I finally agreed.

The weekend turned out to be wonderful. Santa Cruz is where I decided I wanted to spend the rest of my life with Steve Gallagher. I fell in love with him there, although actually I think I already loved him. We immediately moved in together when we returned home on Sunday.

Once again, life seemed full of promise. Kathy was so perfect for me. Her light-hearted and fun-loving personality contrasted with my intensity and seriousness. She was decent, unselfish and friendly—just the kind of girl I could spend the rest of my life with. I occasionally spoke to her about Christianity, which to my delight she was open to hear about. I was sounding her out for the future but didn't want to rush things. Her divorce wasn't final yet, and I knew if she became a Christian she would want to move out.

In spite of the fact that I really liked her, we began having problems. As time went on, my difficult, demanding nature surfaced. I became increasingly irritated with the way she did things and constantly complained about petty annoyances. I attempted to change her through the force of my dominating personality. Although she was easygoing by nature, my continual negative criticism provoked her to respond in anger.

By the end of summer our relationship had really gone

down the tube. One night I came home from work and found a note from her indicating that she had left me. In it, she told me that a Baptist minister had led her into salvation and that she couldn't stay with me any longer. It wasn't until later that I found out that Kathy had experienced a powerful salvation, and she was now deeply committed to serve God with all her heart.

However, this was only part of why she left. The truth was that I was impossible to live with and I knew it. I felt hopeless because I was fully aware that the problem was my miserable, abrasive nature. Even after all these years, I still wanted to serve God and be married to a Christian girl, but that dream seemed absolutely unattainable.

Instead of turning to the Lord, I plunged back into sexual sin. Being involved in real estate allowed me to interact a lot with different people—including young girls. However, once again, my main attention was directed toward easy sex in porn shops and massage parlors.

In the fall of 1979, interest rates began to climb and real estate sales declined. I kept pressing ahead, working harder to maintain the sales momentum necessary to survive in the field of real estate sales.

One September evening, Kathy called me. Her zeal to witness about the Lord to everybody she knew motivated the telephone call. It didn't take long to hear the difference in her voice. It seemed as though she had greatly matured in the few short months since she had moved out of our apartment. She was still Kathy, but there was a discernible solidness of character in her voice that she hadn't possessed when we were together.

"You know, Jesus is coming back soon," she excitedly told me.

"I've been hearing that stuff for ten years," I said with

all of the cynicism of a last-days mocker. Kathy remained calm and friendly, undaunted by my cutting remarks. We talked for a few

Seeing her love for Jesus rekindled my old desires to serve God.

minutes more, but—before she had the chance to say goodbye—I rashly blurted out that she should ask God if it was His will for her to marry me. This suggestion was absolutely outlandish coming from someone so hardhearted and backslidden. Needless to say, she wasn't very receptive to it. The truth is that I was just as surprised by my "proposal" as she was.

Two weeks later, she called me again. After a period of small talk, I took a chance and asked her to go out on a date with me. To my surprise, she agreed.

It was hard to believe the girl sitting in my car was the same one who had previously shacked up with me. When we lived together, she wore blue jeans all the time. Now she was wearing a cotton summer dress that further enhanced the sense of decency she exuded. I was grateful to be with her and genuinely excited about her newfound faith. Seeing her love for Jesus rekindled my old desires to serve God. We enjoyed a relaxing evening together, and she agreed to resume her relationship with me.

On the drive back to her parents' house, she reminded me of my challenge to her to pray about whether she should marry me. "Ever since that night, those words kept coming back to me," she confided. The dating game quickly ended; we decided to get married. In January 1980 we had a simple ceremony in a Baptist church.

Mel and Shirley had also come to the Lord during the summer of 1979, and we all began attending church together. I was unsurrendered however, and unbeknownst to

Although Steve never beat me, I feared him far more than my first husband because his rage seemed to border on insanity.

her, was unfaithful from the very beginning of our marriage. Before long, I gave up any pretense of Christianity and resorted to my former harshness. No matter how hard she tried to please me, she could never make me happy. I was just a miserable person. She describes what it was like being married to me:

> In the beginning, I was very unsure about being married to Steve. While we were dating he was very business-like and intense. I didn't realize until we got married that his business-like manner was simply a cold, lack of emotional involvement with others. His intensity often turned into a rage. Although Steve never beat me, I feared him far more than my first husband because his rage seemed to border on insanity.

In the meantime, my father had also become a Christian, although the lack of change in his life made me skeptical of his conversion. Rather than attend church, looking to be taught and discipled by experienced believers, he immediately began preaching and singing to the patients in a nursing home. Although at one time he had achieved a great deal of personal satisfaction singing in piano bars, now he seemed to derive the same pleasure from singing hymns to the grateful elderly patients attending his services. It was certainly a good thing to do and a great improvement from singing for drunken patrons in a cocktail lounge, but I could never shake the sense that the same selfish desire to be the center of attention motivated him now as it had before.

A major reason for my skepticism was his lack of discernible love for the Lord. He rarely talked about Him or even Christianity *per se* for that matter. Instead, he had become obsessed with right-wing conspiracy theories about powerful politicians and bankers who wanted to rule the world. Any study of the Bible seemed to revolve around digging up proof to support his theories. When Kathy and I would visit him—he had divorced my mother some years prior to this—he always seemed to get the conversation around to these bankers who were plotting to create a one-world government.

On one particular visit, I left the house for a few minutes to see a friend. In the meantime, he had cornered Kathy into a discussion—actually a monologue was more like it. She was a simple girl who had no understanding or interest in such matters. After we left his house that day, she shared with me how uncomfortable it had made her feel.

On my next visit with him, I attempted to talk to him about the way he would "button-hole" her. As humbly and gently as I could, I tried to explain to him how it affected her. "Tell the little b—— not to come around here anymore if she doesn't like it!" he retorted. His words cut deeply, and I simply sighed and dropped the matter.

On another occasion—while he was railing on about the "one-worlders"—I sincerely told him, "Jesus said that we should love our enemies."

"You wouldn't know love if it reached up and bit you in the a—!" he lashed out venomously. I flushed with anger and started toward him. He wisely retreated into the house.

My father quit drinking temporarily when he became a "Christian," but soon he was back to drinking his customary two or three martinis every evening. It was hard to see how

With my past, I saw getting hired as a deputy as a long shot.

he had changed at all. He maintained this habit for the rest of his life.

In 1991, he developed emphysema and spent the last two years of his life gasping for oxygen fed to him through a respirator. One day, he had to be rushed to the hospital because he was unable to breath. Tragically, he was an alcoholic to the end—his body strapped to a gurney, convulsing with DT's in the intensive care unit. He was in a coma when I made it to the hospital, his head swollen beyond recognition. The sight of this pathetic, prideful man in such a terrible condition left me in tears. In spite of the fact that he never sought it—nor did he see a reason to—the Lord helped me to forgive him for the way he treated me my entire life. I held no unforgiveness toward him when he died.

The real estate market suffered a terrible recession in 1980. I had earned good money, but it was quickly running out. The interest rates had skyrocketed and finding good buyers became increasingly more difficult. In less than two years, I had earned and spent over $60,000—a lot of money in those days. By the end of 1980 things were looking very bleak for me financially.

It was obvious I would have to find another line of work. One day, I was talking to my oldest half-sister, Jeannette— my father's daughter from a previous marriage. She was a deputy on the Los Angeles Sheriff's Department. "Steve, the department is aggressively recruiting," she excitedly told me. "Why don't you give it a shot? It can't hurt to try!"

With my past, I saw getting hired as a deputy as a long

shot. Nevertheless, at her insistence, I filled out the twelve-page application and sent it off. Within a couple of months I traveled to Los Angeles to take the written and oral examinations. I passed them both.

I was excited at the prospect of being hired, but I knew the most difficult obstacle in the process still lay before me: the criminal background check. There was no way I would get hired if I admitted the truth to them about my troubled teenage years. Although there were various arrests on my record, I knew that they in themselves weren't enough to disqualify me.

I was finally called in to take a polygraph test. After hooking me up to the lie detector, the interrogator began asking me numerous random questions. When he was done, he told me that the examination indicated that my answers weren't completely honest. However, I stuck to my story and, since he couldn't prove that I was lying about anything, there was nothing he could do about it.

It started to look like I would be hired. I was really out of shape physically and knew that I needed to prepare myself for the physical demands of the sheriff's academy. One evening, I went out jogging and accidentally fell sideways on my left ankle. It quickly became swollen and Kathy drove me to the hospital.

I explained my situation to the doctor and waited for the x-ray results. "Well, it's not broken," the doctor informed me. "But it is a severe sprain and may take months to heal back to normal. In fact, it probably would have healed quicker if it would have been broken." We drove back to Sacramento with my foot propped up on ice. It was two weeks before I could even hobble on it, but I began forcing myself to walk on it, ready or not.

Hopeful that I'd be hired, Kathy and I decided to move

I couldn't believe that I, of all people, was about to become a cop.

to Los Angeles. Not long after arriving there, I was called in to take a physical exam. Part of the assessment involved a stress test. I was required to ride a stationary bicycle for the purpose of determining how hard my cardiovascular system had to work in a given amount of physical effort. After finishing the test, the technician asked me if he could be frank with me.

"Yes, of course," I replied.

"I've been testing guys going into the academy for a long time. There's no way you can make it in the shape you're in."

"I'll make it," I responded confidently.

I'm afraid I wasn't as confident as I sounded. Years of smoking cigarettes and marijuana had deteriorated my lungs. Compounding the problem was the fact that I couldn't run to get myself in better shape. Nevertheless, I was determined to make it through.

One morning in May 1981, a lady from the Sheriff's Department called and told me to report for duty on Monday morning. I simply couldn't believe that I, of all people, was about to become a cop.

That Monday morning I drove downtown to the Hall of Justice in bumper-to-bumper traffic. I made it just in time, and reported to the fourth floor where there were about twenty other people waiting. One of the officers gave us a little talk and then each of us was called into a separate room individually. A lady met me there and told me to raise my right hand and repeat after her. Without any feeling, she rattled off an oath whereby I promised to uphold the law and be prepared at all times to protect the citizens of the United States. I was given a wallet with a badge and an identification card in it and was told to proceed to the Criminal Courts Building for my first assignment as a bailiff: an excellent position for a trainee.

The 19-story Criminal Courts Building was located a block away in downtown Los Angeles. Upon reporting for duty, a deputy named Pete gave me a tour of the building, eventually ending in a long corridor that runs behind the courtrooms, hidden from the public eye. A number of inmates wearing blue jumpsuits stood in line. I was surprised to see a girl in line with the men. "Pete, why's that girl in with those men?" I whispered. He laughed and said, "That girl is a man. He's a transvestite."

Pete took me down to the seventh floor where we sat in on a child custody hearing for a few minutes. They were questioning the father about beating his kids. He was denying everything, but the prosecutor was zeroing in.

"Isn't it true, Mr. Hernandez, that on January fifth 1981, you became furious with your son Jimmie because he had wet the bed, and you beat him with your fists which left bruises and welts on his face?"

"No, sir."

"Let the record show that I have people's exhibit number five. It is a document from El Monte Community Hospital stating that one Jimmie Hernandez was treated for numerous bruises and lacerations on his face on January fifth 1981. Could you explain to the court how Jimmie received these injuries, Mr. Hernandez?"

"As I told the doctor, he fell down the stairway that day."

I was becoming enthralled with the case, but Pete leaned over and whispered that we had to go. We quietly slipped out of the courtroom and made our way up to the fifteenth floor where I spent the rest of the day as a backup to the officer working that courtroom.

For the next three months, I worked as a bailiff in a number of interesting, high-profile felony cases. For instance, Joe Morgan, the notorious head of the Mexican Mafia was on trial for ordering the murder of a drug dealer. Another famous trial going on at that time was that of Angelo Bueno and Kenneth Bianchi, known as the Hillside Stranglers.* Undoubtedly, it was a fascinating assignment. Before I knew it, my three-month assignment there was completed. The following day I had to report to the Los Angeles Sheriff's Academy. I had no comprehension for what awaited me there.

---

* Some years later, the O.J. Simpson trial would be held there.

Four

LOS ANGELES SHERIFF'S ACADEMY

I drove up the long driveway of the academy situated in the rolling hills of East Los Angeles. Even at seven o'clock in the morning, the summer heat could already be felt. The fear and anxiety I had over my first day in the academy left me with butterflies in my stomach. I had been warned about how tough it would be.

At approximately 7:20 I pulled into the parking lot along with many others. A uniformed cadet approached us and told us to put our briefcases in our left hands, keep our mouths shut and follow him. He then led us into a large classroom. The head drill instructor was seated at his desk in the rear. While there were other deputies there also, his menacing glare caused him to stand out. I quickly looked away and sat in the small classroom desk I was directed to.

There must have been over a hundred people already seated. They all looked straight ahead, motionless, and with their hands on their laps—a room full of robots. The silence was eerie and unnerving. At any rate, I followed everyone's example and sat completely still. Reporting time was 7:30. People continued to march in and sit down right

> *I don't know which was worse: the pain, the boredom or the anticipation of what was to come.*

up to the last minute. I looked at the other cadets who I could see without moving my head. Most had taken the time, as I had, to get short, tapered haircuts. The girls had their hair in buns. The look on their faces betrayed the fact that they had been as sobered by the situation as I had.

After we'd sat there for about fifteen minutes, my back began to ache. It wasn't the hard seat that caused the pain, but the fact that my back and leg muscles had to remain tense to keep from sliding down the plastic seat. I don't know which was worse: the pain, the boredom or the anticipation of what was to come. "How much longer can this last?" I wondered.

At about five minutes before eight, I heard the door open and close. A few minutes later, a Mexican-American cadet in a brown suit walked to the front of the classroom and stood at attention, facing the rest of us. After another ten minutes, one of the drill instructors finally came to the front of the classroom. "Cadet Luna, what time were you told to be here this morning?"

"Sir, I was told to be here at 7:30."

"And what time did you get here, Luna?" the D.I. asked in a mockingly nice tone of voice.

"Sir, I got here at approximately eight o'clock," the cadet answered in a monotone voice.

The deputy continued, his voice retaining the same mock kindness. "Cadet Luna, would you please explain to these people why you got here so late?"

"I'm late because I..... "

"Louder, Luna!" A voice boomed from the back of the

classroom. "The people in the back want to hear your lame excuse, too!"

"I'm late because I had a flat tire," he screeched.

"Is that as loud as you can talk, dummy?" It was the sole female deputy speaking now.

"No, sir, I mean ma'am," he responded. He was clearly overwhelmed and confused now.

Seizing the opportunity, the other six D.I.'s rushed to the front of the classroom. "Does she look like a sir to you, clown?" the first deputy roared.

"No, sir," the shaken cadet stammered.

"You're never going to make it through this academy," the drill instructor yelled. "Why don't you just pick up your little briefcase and leave?"

"Sir, I'd like to stay." His courage was admirable.

"Well, you'd better start taking this academy seriously, mister!"

With that, the instructors slowly made their way to the back of the classroom. Luna was doing a commendable job of maintaining his composure. The show was over momentarily, and it was time to sit and wait again. After another twenty minutes or so, another voice boomed from the back. "Class Sergeant, get back here!" He briskly walked to the back of the classroom.

Luna was out of my line of vision for a few minutes before he returned to the front. My back and legs were so cramped by now that I was afraid I wouldn't be able to get out of my desk when the time came. In front of the row nearest the left wall, there was a desk, sitting sideways, facing the other cadets. The beleaguered cadet walked to this desk and slid his briefcase under it. Now it was his turn to give the orders. "Class, a-ten-hut!" The relief swept through my muscles as we exploded out of our chairs. We had been sitting at attention for over an hour and a half and anything had to be an improvement to that. Now that he had our full, undivided attention, he continued. "Class, upon my command you will, uh, leave this class and, uh, stand at attention...."

"Is that what I told you to say, dummy?" It was the voice from the back again.

"Sir, no sir!" he screeched.

"Get 'em down and do it over, Class Sergeant!"

"Sir, yes sir," he responded. "Class, seats!" We all dropped into our seats except the Class Sergeant, who continued to stand at attention. "Class, a-ten-hut!" Again, we sprang to our feet. There were a zillion details to remember in the instructions he was told to give us. We sat down and got up at least a dozen times. If they didn't make him do it over because he fouled up the instructions, it was because we didn't all get up in perfect unison. After approximately a half an hour of this, the deputy that had done most of the yelling at Luna went to the front of the classroom. He wasn't tall, but had broad shoulders.

"Since you're obviously too dumb to handle this simple assignment, I'm going to do it for you." He used a deep, husky voice to issue the command. "Class, a-ten-hut!" Once again, everyone jumped up, but this time in unison. "Class, upon my command, you will fall out of this classroom and onto the grinder in a marching formation, south of the solid white line, facing north. Fall out!" Most of us had no idea what a marching formation was, and nobody in his right mind dared to ask.

Once we got outside, the instructors showed us that a marching formation was four columns deep with the tallest people at one end and the shortest at the other end. They told us to take a look at the people around us so we could remember where we belonged in line. After everyone did this, they called us by name and arranged us alphabetically in platoon formation. I was assigned to the third platoon. Deputy

I had been informed that the way to survive was to blend in. The ones that stood out would bear the brunt of the attack.

Sennett walked up to us and explained that he was to be our platoon officer. He showed us how to line up. The biggest guys were placed in the front and the smallest in the back. There were about seven to a line, with four lines in a platoon. I was placed in the third line. That was fine with me; I could hide easier in the back. I had been informed that the way to survive was to blend in. The ones that stood out would bear the brunt of the attack.

Deputy Sennett didn't look like a cop, let alone a drill instructor. He wasn't particularly big, and he certainly wasn't "macho" looking, like most of the other D.I.s. As a matter of fact, he had an innocent looking baby face.

We spent another hour going back and forth in formations until we got it right. All the while, they were screaming at us. "You're the slowest, dumbest class we've ever had in this academy! This may be the first time a whole class gets fired!" On and on they went. We were either standing at attention or running to stand at attention. My back had never ached so badly.

The rest of the day was spent doing similar things. At 7:30 p.m., we were given an assignment to type a two-page autobiography and were dismissed for the night.

I didn't get home until 8:15. I needed a typewriter, but the only possibility was Kathy's office. While I stayed behind to write the story, she raced downtown to her office. Fortunately, a night guard was there to let her in. When she returned, she couldn't type a full page without making errors. I was completely exhausted and stressed out over the day's events. I got mad every time she made a mistake. "Can't you type a simple little piece of paper?" I stormed. The angrier I became, the harder it was for her to type it correctly. It was 2:30 in the morning before we completed it.

At 5:45 I was back on the road. I had my briefcase, gym clothes, autobiography and two hours of sleep. Again, as we arrived, cadets from the other class were awaiting us in the parking lot, logging our arrivals. At exactly 7:30, we were standing in platoon formation for the raising of the flag.

This was our first encounter with the sergeant, who was even more intimidating than the deputies. The sergeant barked out his orders. "A-ttention to colors... present, arms!"

As he said "arms," we were to salute the flag. About half the people saluted and the other half put their hands on their hearts. As the flag was being raised, a tape recording of a horn playing reveille was played over the loudspeaker. When the music was over, the sergeant faced us and barked, "Or-der, arms!" Half of the class snapped their hands back to their sides while the other half stood there not knowing what to do. It was a poor example of uniformity.

Now it was time for the first inspection. Each drill instructor went to the front of his platoon and carefully inspected each individual. People were being yelled at on both sides of me. One of the cadets named Adams was in the first platoon—handled by the head drill instructor. Adams slightly resembled the Pillsbury Doughboy. I listened to their conversation as I awaited my own inspection.

"Adams, I've just had a vision of what you must look like in the nude!"

"Yes, sir."

"Adams, did you brush your teeth this morning?"

"Yes, sir."

"Well, your breath smells like a dead cat!"

"Yes, sir."

I picked out a spot on the hillside to stare at—just a little higher than my D.I.'s eye level. And then there he was.

On and on he went. Some of his remarks were hilarious, but I couldn't even entertain the thought of laughter. In the meantime, my own drill inspector was getting closer to me as he made his way through my platoon. I wondered how well I would hold up when he started in on me. I picked out a spot on the hillside to stare at—just a little higher than my D.I.'s eye level. And then there he was.

"Gallagher, are you married to an old Indian squaw?"

"Sir?"

"I asked you if you're married to an old Indian squaw," he repeated irritably.

"No, sir."

"Those pants look like an old Indian squaw took 'em down to the river and beat 'em on the rocks!" I never have been a neat dresser.

"Yes, sir."

"Well, are you married?"

"Yes, sir."

"Is she a heavy equipment operator?"

"No, sir."

As quickly as he came, he moved on to the next guy. We must have stood at attention for two hours. The bottoms of my heels were killing me. My lower back and calf muscles were aching and cramping. Then it happened. Some guy in another platoon fell straight forward like a felled tree. He landed right on his face. We stayed at attention. The depu-

> *I feared physical training more than any other aspect of the academy. My lungs were in poor condition, and I had no idea if my ankle would hold up.*

ties ran over and hauled him off. An ambulance showed up a while later. His jaw had been shattered, and he had to be recycled into a later class. He had made the mistake of locking his knees, which cut off the circulation to his calves. A lack of blood flow to his brain caused him to pass out.

Finally, Luna attempted to give us orders again. "Class, upon my command you will fall out of this platoon formation and fall into the locker room...."

"You big dummy!" It was the female deputy. "Do you want the female cadets to change in the same locker room as yours?"

"No, ma'am!" he responded crisply.

"We're getting sick and tired of you, Luna!" she barked.

"Get it done, Luna!" one of the male D.I.'s piped in.

"Sir, yes sir! Class, upon my command you will fall out of this platoon formation and into your respective locker rooms where you will change from your suits into your P.T. gear. Fall out!"

It was a mad dash into the locker room which was obviously made to fit about 40 people at one time, not 150! Somehow, everyone managed to get changed and lined up in the gymnasium. I feared physical training more than any other aspect of the academy. My lungs were in poor condition, and I had no idea if my ankle would hold up. Our P.T. instructor was a big ex-marine named Deputy Harris. He got started once we were all lined up.

"Half-right, face! Push up position, move!" We did twenty slow push-ups, then twenty sit-ups, twenty push-ups, twenty burpees, twenty push-ups and then fifteen leg lifts. Then we did it all over again—only this time, the tempo was escalated.

Finally, we were taken for a long run through the side streets and alleys of East Los Angeles. The difficult part of the course was that we had to run in perfect step and yell cadence as we ran. After running several miles, people began passing out. Somehow I managed to keep going, one step at a time. Sweat poured into my eyes, burning them so much that I could hardly see. I learned to squint to limit the amount of sweat that got into them. Although the California sun was beating down on us, chills ran up and down my spine. My ankle ballooned to twice its normal size, and every step brought a wince of pain. However, I did my best not to limp because if they knew how bad it was, they would remove me from the academy until my ankle got better. Eventually, we were led back to the gym where we did more calisthenics. After a quick shower, we were returned to the classroom where we finished out the day.

They released us about 5:30 that evening. I couldn't imagine being able to take this for eighteen more weeks, but I was determined to make it. Others didn't share my resolve. The guy who stood next to me in my platoon told me, "I really don't need this! I can make just as much money back in my old job. I'm quitting!" Indeed, over twenty cadets resigned during that first week. This was exactly what the directors of the academy wanted. They made the first two weeks extremely difficult—and purposely conveyed the false impression that it would be that hard throughout the entire length of the academy.

The truth was that it became easier as time went on. The emphasis gradually shifted from drill and discipline to scholastic and practical training. We were taught about first aid, safety, the elements of different crimes and policing techniques. Detectives who handled homicide, child abuse, vice and narcotics gave lectures about their respective fields. We also watched movies about officer survival and dramatizations of events which led to the actual deaths of several deputies. We were taught that the will to live must be the most important thing in every officer's mind. "Kick, bite, punch or scratch, but don't let some dirt-bag leave you to die in a gutter somewhere!" we were dramatically instructed.

About halfway through the academy, we started going out on patrol with deputies in the various sheriff substations around the county. On one of these occasions I was allowed to work out of Firestone—one of the "hottest" stations in the county. This was located in a section of South Central Los Angeles that bordered the Watts. I was told that I would be working the early morning shift and was to report for duty at midnight.

Just as I was being assigned to my partner, a middle-aged Latino man with a bleeding hand ran into the station. He yelled in broken English, "Two guys come into bar with guns and I shoot them, bang, bang!" He had a broad smile on his face as he excitedly recounted the story. "One shot me in hand, but I shot him!"

We jumped in our squad car and raced to the bar. The guy had been an excellent shot. One man had been rushed to the hospital with a gunshot to the groin. The other guy lay dead on the sidewalk, his head in a pool of blood. Two patrol cars blocked off the scene and awaited the homicide detectives, crime lab technicians and the coroner. I was fascinated with the scene but had to remain at a distance so that no evidence would be damaged.

We spent the rest of the night racing from one call to

the next. Peace officers are only supposed to break traffic laws when they have permission to go "code three" with lights and siren. How-

You never know who has a gun, so you have to be more aggressive.

ever, ghetto cops often become addicted to the excitement. We flew through red lights and stop signs as if they weren't even there. I was told that they called it "in-car code three." We handled everything from assault with a deadly weapon to a lady on P.C.P. "Calls are handled differently in the ghetto, than in stations in the suburbs," my partner informed me. "You never know who has a gun, so you have to be more aggressive." We rolled back into the station parking lot a few minutes before 8 a.m. It had been a long but interesting night.

We had a lot of fun during our last week of the academy. By this point, a third of the original class of 150 cadets had quit under pressure. It seemed that the instructors were satisfied that they "washed out" those they didn't consider "cop material." The deputies were now much more casual. Friday was our big day. We donned our dressy uniforms for the graduation ceremony to be held at the civic center. A rush of pride surged through me as I stepped to the front to receive my certificate from Sheriff Peter Pitchess.

Going through the sheriff's academy had a profound impact on my life. Unquestionably, the training boosted my confidence as a young man. Having completed this grueling course in spite of so many obstacles gave me the sense that I could accomplish whatever I set my mind to do. It also birthed in me a sense of self-discipline that would later become a very important element of my life.

The sheriff's academy transformed me from a civilian to a bona fide cop. However, before I could become a patrol deputy, I had to serve my stint at the county jail. I received my assignment: Wayside Max!

Five

Maximum Security!

I was assigned to the maximum-security facility at Wayside Honor Rancho.* That Monday morning I left our apartment in Sherman Oaks and made the 25-mile trip north on Interstate 5 to Castaic Junction. During the drive, I recalled how the drill instructor had warned us that we would have to prove ourselves before the other deputies would accept us. In spite of all my bravado, my secret concern was whether or not I had what it took to function in such a rough environment. The Los Angeles County jail system housed some of the most ruthless criminals in the country. I had been assigned—not to medium or minimum security—but to a maximum-security facility. Although I had performed much better than I had expected in the academy, this would be the real thing.

I left the freeway and made my way up to the front entrance of the compound. I pulled my new Camaro alongside the booth at the main gate and explained to the guard that I was scheduled to start that day. He im-

* This was later renamed the Peter J. Pitchess Center.

patiently waved me through the gate.

Driving the four miles through the compound up to Maximum, I noticed the self-sufficiency of the ranch. There were at least a hundred acres of crops, a dairy, a hog farm, a laundry and a bakery. I drove through the Minimum complex where the low risk inmates lived in barracks. Then I arrived at Max.

It was a large, foreboding building painted with a sickening cream color. After parking my car, I entered the structure and noticed the huge sliding gate that led into the actual jail portion of the building. Standing along a wall were the familiar faces of a number of my classmates from the academy. It was such a relief to see men I knew. We sat down at the long table in the briefing room and quietly awaited instructions. Once everyone had arrived and was seated, a man walked to the front of the room and introduced himself as Deputy Conrad.

He spent the entire morning describing the layout of the building and discussing what our duties would be. Conrad explained that there were twelve dorms which housed approximately 100 inmates each. Some of these dormitories contained pre-sentenced inmates who were considered more dangerous than the others. Many were looking at long prison terms. There were six dorms upstairs and six downstairs. There were also disciplinary modules that contained two-man cells, as well as two solitary cells ominously called "the hole."

After lunch we took a tour of the place. As we passed through the first two gates, I noticed how long the building was. The main hall stretched over a hundred and fifty yards. We made our way upstairs where six of the dormitories were located. An officer's passageway ran the length of the building in front of the dormitories. A chain link fence with a sliding gate was all that kept the inmates inside. In the passageway of each dorm was a dorm officer's desk. What accosted my ears was the incredible level of noise. The inmates had turned the volume of each television

Dorm 331 was notoriously known as the "queen tank," holding approximately 70 homosexuals.

set as high as it could go, so it could be heard over the clamor of yelling inmates. It was a deafening raucous.

At 4 p.m. the next day, I returned to work on the night shift—where most of the action occurred. I was assigned to work dorms 331 and 332. Dorm 331 was notoriously known as the "queen tank," holding approximately 70 homosexuals. I stood there staring in utter disbelief. I had never seen anything like this before.

The dayshift officer snapped me back from my thoughts. "Here are the keys. The book, board and wheel are balanced in both dorms. Everything's been quiet today. See ya' later."

I took the keys from him but had no idea what he was talking about, and it was anything but quiet. I walked over to dorm 332 and sat down in front of the security screen. Immediately I was inundated with requests:

"Deputy, can I have some aspirins?"

"Deputy, can I get some tobacco?"

"Deputy, can I get on the phone list?"

As I tried to determine what requests I should agree to, a message came over the PA system. Unfortunately, I couldn't make it out because of all the noise and commotion. The whole building could have been overrun with rioting inmates, and I wouldn't have known it. I decided to spend my time in front of the quieter "queen tank." As I leaned against the desk, a skinny, black transvestite sauntered over to me. "Dep-u-tee," he purred, "may I have some aspirins, please?" He thrust his right hip out and put his hand on it, making what I suppose must have been his sexiest pose. I gave him two aspirins through the security screen and watched him saunter away.

It didn't take long for me to settle into the routine of a dorm officer, but I soon began longing to become one of the "prowlers." This was a team of deputies who handled various tasks in the jail, including any emergencies that might arise. Whenever a problem arose, an announcement would go over the PA system and the prowlers would rush to respond. These emergencies usually involved either an inmate provoking a deputy or fighting amongst prisoners.

In spite of the fact that I still harbored a lot of fear inside, I had come out of the academy well trained and ready for action. In a strange sort of way, my anxieties actually made me more aggressive. Anxious to prove myself to my new comrades, I began responding to those emergency calls myself. In no time I had developed a reputation in the jail as someone the other deputies could count on.

The inmates were similar to kids in that they would try and get away with as much as the deputies allowed. They would test each officer to see how far they could push him. There were some deputies who the prisoners took advantage of because they lacked the inner strength to stand up to them.

I got along fairly well with the inmates even though I was one of the more aggressive deputies. My one big advantage over most of the other deputies was that I was already street-wise before joining the department. Having grown up in the criminal element, I knew how these men thought and for the most part was not intimidated by them.

However, I was by no means the perfect deputy. The

best officers, as I saw it, were those who were able to do their job without letting things bother them. If inmates said something provoking, they would sim-

Working in the jail became a way of life for me. I was addicted to the excitement.

ply respond according to the "book." I often lacked the maturity to handle things this way and would sometimes react out of anger. My hot temper occasionally caused me to be reckless.

One night I was in the back of one of the pre-sentence dorms by myself. The dorm deputy stood outside the gate, but he could not enter under any circumstances. There must have been thirty inmates in that dormitory facing murder charges. As I started toward the front, one of them made some derogatory remark about me. Usually, I would simply ignore it, but I was in a nasty mood that day. I didn't have any idea who it was, but I turned around and challenged any one of them to fight me right then and there. It was a very foolish, reckless and immature thing for me to do. Fortunately no one responded. I could have been badly hurt or even killed. Many of those inmates were facing long prison sentences and—since there was no death penalty in California at that time—had nothing to lose. Indeed, killing a deputy would enable a man to go to prison with the respected title of "cop killer."

Working in the jail became a way of life for me. I looked forward to work each day. I was addicted to the excitement, and after several months as a dorm officer, I finally became a prowler. That was so much better than sitting in front of a dorm for eight hours straight. There were many responsibilities, but I was no longer confined to one spot all night.

The best part of it was being able to respond to distur-

It's hard to say what would have happened to us had those deputies continued to follow me into that volatile atmosphere.

bances. One night some deputies took an inmate out of a dorm and gave him a hard time. He had been pressuring smaller inmates to give him their possessions. After they finished with him, they put him back into the dorm.

I was at the front desk in the office when the emergency call came through. The prisoner was going berserk in the dormitory—yelling and kicking a garbage can around. Although I was supposed to remain at my post at the front, I rushed to the dorm and arrived at the same time as a few other deputies. We all gave our keys to the dorm officer and rushed in. As the inmate retreated to the back of the huge room, all of the other inmates started yelling for us to leave him alone. As we hesitated to go after him, inmates started jumping out of their beds to confront us. I turned around to find the other officers had wisely headed back out the gate, leaving me there by myself. I was furious with them for backing down from the inmates. As I walked out, an older deputy calmly walked in with all of the bearing of a lieutenant and led the inmate out without incident. It's hard to say what would have happened to us had those deputies continued to follow me into that volatile atmosphere super-charged with so much hatred. Once again, in spite of my rebellion, God continued to watch over me.

After a few months in the jail, I put in for a transfer to the Carson Sheriff Substation, where Jeannette's husband Gil worked as a lieutenant. I began riding patrol on some of my off nights, hoping to familiarize myself with the streets while awaiting my transfer. This station not only covered the city of Carson but also extended up into the ghetto areas adjacent to Firestone and the Watts. It was a fast paced station with a lot of action, and yet it didn't have the macho mentality found in ghetto stations.

I was riding with another guy one night, when we got a call to back up another unit on a burglary-in-progress call. We raced the twenty or so blocks to the scene and parked on the street behind the house. I had wanted to go straight to the house, but my partner had correctly guessed that the burglars would come out the back way. We were parked at the end of the street when I spotted them. Three Hispanics were running toward the street from between two houses. My partner sped down there in the squad car, and I jumped out while it was still moving. I grabbed two of them and threw them into a fence and told them to put their hands behind their heads. The third took off running with my partner right behind him in the car. As inexperienced as I was, I hadn't thought to pull my gun out. As I patted them down for weapons, another unit showed up. It turned out all right, but it was another example of my recklessness.

———

If my law enforcement career was on track, my marriage wasn't. I loved Kathy—at least as well as I could at that time—but I was getting increasingly dissatisfied with being tied down to marriage. I was torn in two opposite directions. On one hand, I wanted to settle down with my wife and even get back on track with God again. Unfortunately, the cop life was continually pushing me in the other direction of wanting excitement and freedom.

As usual, sex was constantly on my mind. It wasn't too much of a problem during the academy simply because my

I explained that he was a famous porn star and asked her if she would like to see one of his movies. To my astonishment, she agreed.

every waking moment was dominated by thoughts of survival. However, once I started settling into my job in the jail, the old desires began to resurface. I started frequenting adult bookstores and massage parlors again.

However, Kathy was trying to make our marriage work. We had been married for only two years, and she had long since given up following the Lord. What had once been a fiery love for God had now become an ember that was about to be completely extinguished. She too had been pulled in two different directions: serving the Lord or pleasing her husband. I didn't want to be a Christian and, at that point in her walk with God, she was simply too weak to stand on her own. Gradually, she slid away from God until she finally gave up all pretenses of being a Christian.

One night, I mentioned to her that John Holmes was in our jail. She asked me who he was. I explained that he was a famous porn star and asked her if she would like to see one of his movies. To my astonishment, she agreed. We bought a video recorder—a brand new invention—and began renting X-rated movies. These weren't the silent 8-mm films I had watched in the adult bookstores but high quality, full-length motion pictures with story lines and scripts. This new branch of the entertainment world had its own producers, directors, camera crews, stars and starlets. Nearly every imaginable fantasy was portrayed in vivid scenes. This new industry also had its own culture and values, which were loudly conveyed in every movie. The sex-is-everything mindset communicated by these motion pictures deepened my obsession with illicit sex. It also broke down many of Kathy's inhibitions.

She shares her perspective of that time:

> I never dreamed in a thousand years I would stoop to watching people have sex on film, but the years I had been with Steve were preparing me for this. I could see a spark in Steve's eye when he asked me about watching these movies. I saw that the more interest I showed in pornography, the more interest Steve showed in me.
>
> When he told me about the movies, I experienced a mixed reaction. It crushed me to think I had to compete with the women in those films and magazines. Unfortunately, instead of turning to God with my pain, I tried harder to please Steve. The other side to it was that he started treating me better than ever before.
>
> My pursuit for his love and affection grew more intense. Some days it seemed that my heart would literally burst from the pain and rejection. When he was sweet to me though, I would hold out hope that he would change. I allowed the pornography to continue because he assured me that it would enhance our sex lives and improve our relationship.

As Kathy and I began watching these movies, I found that it was much easier to talk to her. The illicit culture expressed in the videos altered our perspectives of marriage, lovemaking and even life itself. What was once a natural expression of physical intimacy—only one aspect of many that make up a marriage—was now magnified into the centerpiece of our relationship. I looked forward to the weekends when a pornographic video would serve as the highlight to our own private sex party.

This mutual mindset emboldened me to tell her about my visits to prostitutes and massage parlors. I was oblivious to her feelings and never considered how this would affect her. It relieved me to be honest with her, and I convinced myself that I'd done the right thing. But the truth was that it crushed her emotionally.

Initially I was very excited when we started watching movies together. I actually started treating her with kindness. However, it wasn't long before I became dissatisfied again. As that happened, my anger surfaced once again. I constantly berated and verbally abused her. I was utterly self-absorbed and had no comprehension for how beaten down she was as a person. Unbeknownst to me, she had finally reached her limit:

> Steve was such an angry man all the time. He was just impossible to please. I had allowed him to have the pornography he wanted so desperately and now he became crueler than ever before. He was completely obsessed with his job and poured his heart and soul into it. I respected him for his dogged determination but resented having to become even lower on his list of priorities.

> One time, during an argument, Steve told me, "You are getting as much from me as you are going to get. If you're not happy with what you have, go somewhere else." He went on to say that I was ungrateful and should be happy to have him as a husband. I had always

"I don't need Steve Gallagher to survive in life," I told myself. "In fact, if I don't leave I won't survive!"

looked up to Steve and I believed what he said. I tried to be more grateful for him, but I soon realized that guys with that attitude came a dime a dozen.

A deep resentment began to build in me that eventually replaced the sense that I couldn't live without him. I started thinking that I would rather be single the rest of my life than to stay married to him. This conviction grew over several months until I finally decided to leave him and go back to my family in Sacramento. "I don't need Steve Gallagher to survive in life," I told myself. "In fact, if I don't leave I won't survive!"

Six

THE LONGEST SIX HOURS

It had been a fairly typical night at the jail, with the exception of the inmate who had raped a fellow cellmate. "That dirt-bag will pay for this, even if our judicial system won't do anything about it!" I thought to myself, before I picked a fight with him. Dispensing my own brand of justice became a way of life for me. Yes, I was a seasoned prowler on the loose.

I was also doing a lot more drinking, especially nights like this when I had been involved in some action. A few of us went out that night and drank a case of beer. Many nights we would either go to a local country-western bar or would pick up some beer and hang out at the apartment of one of the guys.

This particular night I got home some time after 2:00 a.m. My heart sank as I opened the door to the apartment. Lying on the floor in front of the door was a note from my wife. I grabbed the scrap of paper and read it. She said that she was sorry to hurt me like this but just couldn't take anymore. Of course, this came as a complete shock because, in my delusion, I had imagined that our marriage was fine. The only thing that stood out in my mind at that moment was how poorly I had treated her.

I was very upset and yet felt helpless to get her back. Strangely, a part of me was happy about my newfound freedom, even though I still loved her. I felt crushed but sought comfort through other women. Within a few days I had initiated relationships with two different women. Although I missed my wife, I was determined to make the best of the situation.

About a week after Kathy left, I met yet another woman at a party. For the next couple of weeks we became inseparable. I began staying at her place more than my own. Needless to say, Kathy was already fading from my memory.

One Saturday morning, I awoke at this woman's apartment with an unexplainable longing to get Kathy back. Taking into account how well things had been going, this sudden burden seemed out of place. So I called my mother in Sacramento and asked for her advice. She told me that my only hope was to turn my life over to God and to start praying and fasting. "I might consider living as a Christian if Kathy comes back to me, but there's no way I can do it without her," I surmised to her.

"It will never work that way, Steve," she replied.

Her words kept going through my mind that evening at work. The following morning I called Shirley, my mother-in-law. She told me that Kathy had been gone a few days with a "friend." She went on to tell me that the Lord had revealed to her—and to Kathy's sister Linda—that it was His will for our marriage to be restored. Considering the amount of anger they had had toward me, it seemed obvious that God was at work. However, her concluding remark brought me back down to earth: "Steve, I gotta' tell you that Kathy is dead set against ever coming back to you.

In fact, she has filed for divorce." Unbeknownst to me, her "friend" was some guy she had recently met. Kathy explains how she met this man:

> The day after I got to Sacramento my car overheated. So I pulled into a parking lot in front of a bar. I opened up the hood to see what was wrong. As I stood there not knowing what to do, a guy named Tim came out of the bar.
>
> He seemed so kind and genuinely interested in helping me. Once he fixed the problem, he offered to buy me a drink. Accepting a drink from a perfect stranger was not like me, but I was very grateful to him. As we talked, I found myself telling him all about my cop husband in L.A. I had just left. I was amazed to find out that he also lived in the Los Angeles area.
>
> Tim started telling me about a man who could take away all my pain and give me a new life. It soon dawned on me that he was talking about Jesus. It was like a breath of fresh air. I was hungry for the Lord, and—in my confusion and distress—Tim represented Him to me.
>
> He had to return to Los Angeles the next day, but he immediately began sending me flowers. He would call me every day. His sweetness and ability to make me laugh and forget the pain I had been through with Steve blinded me to the fact that he could guzzle a six-pack of beer in one sitting. Although his lifestyle did not represent Christianity, I convinced myself that God had sent him to me. Before I knew it, I was living with him.

At this point, I was still under the illusion that Kathy

was getting away from it all with some girlfriend. Although hearing that she had filed for divorce upset me, for some unexplainable reason my heart became flooded with hope. I decided to stay at home to fast and pray that evening as my mother had advised me.

As we talked, sex with other women suddenly seemed so unimportant to me.

Ten minutes after I got to work the next day, Kathy called. She asked a couple of questions about our taxes but was very cold and distant. She said that she hadn't talked to her mom lately, and I suggested that she should. She made it clear that she was only calling for business purposes.

I was miserable that entire night. Being stationed at the front desk meant that I couldn't eat my supper in the deputy "chow hall" until late. The only deputy still there was a Christian guy named Willie. He could see I was troubled.

"What's wrong, Gallagher?"

I explained the whole situation to him. As we talked, sex with other women suddenly seemed so unimportant to me. "Willie, I don't know what to do," I finally lamented.

"Why don't you ask the Lord to forgive you of your sins and put this whole mess into His hands?" he suggested.

I agreed and bowed my head right there at the table. "Lord, I have been sinful and have rebelled against you. I repent of my sin and ask You to take control of my life once again. Please forgive me of my sins and straighten out my life." It was the first time I had ever really given Him everything. Instantly, I was filled with peace of mind.

The next day, I tried to explain it to my girlfriend, but she couldn't understand. "What does God have to do with us?" she wanted to know. Even though she couldn't understand my reasons, I knew the relationship had to end. In spite of her reaction, this only deepened my sense of peace. However, by the time my shift ended that night, the peace had vanished. The only thing on my mind was how I could win Kathy back. All night long I tossed and turned, crying out to God to send her back to me. In the middle of the night the Lord spoke to me. It was a voice, and yet, it didn't come into my mind through my ears. He said, "She will call you tomorrow."

The next morning I got up around 11:00 a.m. and decided to drive down the street to a fast-food restaurant. "Wait a minute, I can't do that," I thought to myself. "Kathy's going to call." No sooner had this thought entered my mind than I realized that if she was going to call it would be God's doing. He would have her call when I was there. I went to eat and she called about ten minutes after I returned. Kathy describes how it came about that she contacted me:

> Although Tim seemed like Prince Charming to me, I noticed that my thoughts continually returned to Steve. One day, I called him on the pretense of needing information about taxes, but I remained aloof. However, a few days later, I found myself doing a very strange thing. I started driving toward Steve's apartment. It seemed like someone else was driving the car. When I arrived there, I called him from the phone booth down the street.

As soon as she identified herself, I began pouring my heart out to her, explaining to her what had happened to me the night before. "I prayed all night last night and you may not believe this, but God told me you were going to call!" I exclaimed. She was listening but was very noncommittal. "Have you talked to your mom since we talked the other day?" I asked.

"No," she replied.

"Well, why don't you call her up and give me a call back." I had no idea

I didn't want to go back to him, and yet I knew it was the Lord telling me to.

what kind of battle was going on inside her. Kathy reminisces about that day:

I was glad to hear about Steve's new life, but I had no intention of going back to him. My feelings for him were dead. Tim was giving me the love that I had wanted from Steve, and I was becoming accustomed to being treated like a princess. I was convinced that God had given me what I had wanted for so long by bringing Tim into my life. As far as I was concerned, Steve had lost his opportunity. I would be a fool to return to him.

In desperation, Steve challenged me to call my parents for their advice. I was glad to call them because I knew my parents were furious about the way he had treated me. When my dad answered the phone, I explained the situation to him. I was shocked at his response. "Kathy, you need to be home with your husband!" I had never heard such conviction in my dad's voice before. Even though this confirmed that it really was the Lord's will, I was crushed. The last thing I wanted to do was to go back to Steve. I slumped down in that phone booth and sobbed uncontrollably. I didn't want to go back to him, and yet I knew it was the Lord telling me to. I feared being disobedient to the Lord and decided to go back to Steve only because I had to. Finally, after pulling myself back together, I called him back.

The telephone rang a few minutes later. "My parents said that God told them that we should get back together," she told me. "But there's just one problem. I have a boyfriend. Do you want me to come over so we can talk?"

"Yes!"

She arrived a few minutes later and explained what had happened. I was just happy to have her back. We spent the night together. It seemed like old times, although she was very upset because she felt so much guilt about having committed adultery. The next morning she called Tim and told him she was staying with me. She started crying because now she felt guilty about hurting him. He told her that he was packing up and going to San Diego to be with his family. She had to go to the house they had been living in to get her stuff, but we decided that she should wait until later, when he was sure to be gone.

About 12:30 p.m. she called the house to make sure Tim wasn't there. Nobody answered so she left to go over there. As she was getting ready to go, she said, "Steve, pray that I'll have the strength to leave him."

"What do ya' mean by that?" I questioned.

"Nothing," she said as she walked out the door.

She hadn't been gone five minutes when I regretted letting her go. Nothing could be done about it, though. She had refused to give me the address or the phone number. I convinced myself that everything would be all right and went about cleaning up the apartment. Figuring her trip would take about an hour, at 1:30 I walked to the front of the apartment building to watch for her. I stood out there about five minutes waiting, and then it occurred to me that she might try calling. I went back inside and immediately felt an urgency to pray.

I got on my knees next to my bed and thanked God for

all that He had done to bring us back together. I prayed that He would give her strength to leave that house—if she needed it for some reason. Realizing what the Lord had already

It became very clear to me that if she didn't return I would commit suicide. I began shaking in fear for my life.

done brought tears streaming down my cheeks. After about twenty minutes of prayer, I heard the front door close. Relief swept over me that Kathy had returned, but when she didn't come into the bedroom, I went out to investigate. The sickening realization that the wind from an open window had slammed the door shut swept over me. Panic set in. "What was taking her so long? Why didn't she at least call?" I wondered.

I went back on my knees and begged God to send her back to me. "Why did You put us back together, only to allow us to split up again?" I demanded to know. After another half an hour of prayer the phone rang. I answered it, but it was only a dial tone. Suddenly, a foreboding feeling swept over me that I could not survive the night without her. It became very clear to me that if she didn't return I would commit suicide. I began shaking in fear for my life.

Just then I remembered a crumpled piece of paper that was in my pocket. It was the phone number of a pastor I had met at the jail. Not knowing what else to do, I telephoned him and quickly gave him a rundown of the situation. He told me that he didn't have a car right then but would try to get one. As we talked, the operator suddenly cut in on the conversation. "There is an emergency phone call from Kathy. Will you clear the line?" she asked.

"Yes!" I blurted out.

"Praise the Lord, brother," the pastor exclaimed. "That's God working!"

I hung up the phone waiting for her to call. Seconds ticked by and it didn't ring. Several minutes came and went; still no phone call. A dark cloud of despair came upon me, leaving me in such internal anguish that I clenched my teeth tightly and writhed on the floor crying out to God. Jesus said that hell was a place where lost sinners will weep and gnash their teeth, a perfect description of the deep agony which overwhelmed my soul. Nothing could relieve that distress except Kathy's return.

I had been upset and depressed when she had first left me, but this internal torment was something much deeper than the loss of a loved one. I called the pastor again and told him that she hadn't called back. He said he would come over as soon as he could get a car. I didn't know if Tim was holding her against her will or if she had just decided she didn't want to come back to me. "Why, oh why, did I let her leave by herself?" I despaired.

It was about 3:30 when the pastor showed up at the front door—three hours since she had left. Seeing him helped a little. He was only there about two minutes when the phone rang. Kathy describes what she experienced that day:

> I drove over to the house Tim was staying at with a strange fear. "Why should I fear this man who has been so kind to me?" I wondered. "Besides that, he's not even there. He's already down in San Diego by now."
>
> I pulled up to the house and his car wasn't there. The house looked deserted, so I unlocked the door and went in. As soon as I stepped through the front door, I felt a cold, eerie feeling, almost evil. I quickly

made my way back to the bedroom. I just wanted to get my stuff and get out of there. As soon as I opened the door, I was startled to find Tim sitting there

He continued trying to convince me that I shouldn't go back to Steve. The more he talked, the more confused I became.

on the bed. He had a cold, mean look on his face. I had only seen him as friendly and jovial before this.

"How could you even think of going back to him after all you've done to hurt him?" he wanted to know. "Haven't I been all that you ever wanted?" It was as if he could read my mind and all the confusing, conflicting thoughts I was having. He continued trying to convince me that I shouldn't go back to Steve. The more he talked, the more confused I became. I felt like I had already hurt Steve and now I was hurting Tim.

"I know full well what Steve is really like so why should I go back to him," I began to think. Tim vacillated between calm and anger. Finally, in a rage, he forced himself on me. I was so weak and mousey at the time that I let him have his way. In some strange way, it worked to bring me back into Tim's arms again. I finally agreed to call Steve and tell him I wasn't coming back to him.

I tried to call but the phone was busy. I tried again and it was still busy. Finally I called the operator and asked her to break in on the conversation. I just figured Steve didn't want me back and had taken the phone off the hook. As soon as I hung up with the operator, I called right back.

I grabbed my off duty revolver and twirled the cylinder by the mouthpiece of the phone.

The phone rang and rang but nobody answered it. (To this day we can't explain this because that was right when Steve was sitting by the phone anxiously waiting for my call.)

As soon as the pastor arrived, Kathy got through. "Hello!" I answered with great urgency.

"It's me." The cold tone had returned to her voice.

"Where are you, what are you doing?" I wanted to know.

"Steve, I love Tim and I'm not coming back to you."

"You don't love him, you love me! I'm your husband!" I exclaimed.

"Steve, I can't come back."

When she said that, I grabbed my off duty revolver which was sitting on the coffee table and twirled the cylinder by the mouthpiece of the phone. It made a loud click as the cylinder slammed into place. "You hear that? You can just sit there and listen to me blow my brains out!" With that I put the gun to my head. The chaplain began frantically jumping up and down yelling, "Lady, he means it! He's gonna' do it!"

Just then Kathy screamed into the phone, "Steve, don't do it!" When she did that, Tim grabbed her arm and she looked up at him. He looked completely different. Evil permeated his face. It was as if the angel of light was suddenly revealed for who he really was. "Kathy," he sneered at her, "if he wants to kill himself, let him do it. It's not your fault!" Then she realized that this man was no prince; he was full of the devil. When she said that, I pulled the gun away from my head. God had spared me yet again.

Now she understood that she was in the wrong place but

was too frightened to leave and still very confused. The pastor got on the phone and prayed with her. He ordered the spirits of confusion to leave her alone and pleaded for God's intervention. Instantly she knew what she should do. It was a violent struggle of life and death in the spiritual world. I just kept praying, which was all I knew to do.

She was afraid to tell us where she was because he was there in the room, pacing back and forth like a madman. She promised to meet the pastor at his church. So he gave her directions. I got back on the phone and told her that I loved her and that she was forgiven for what had just happened. She said she wanted me to come to the church, too. I agreed and we hung up.

The pastor and I arrived at his church and waited... and waited... and waited. She had given the pastor Tim's phone number after he had promised her that he wouldn't give it to me. I convinced him to call to see if she was all right. He tried, but there was no answer. That made me concerned that maybe she had given him the wrong number. An hour later he called again. This time Tim answered. He told the pastor that Kathy had just left and had taken all her stuff with her. I was somewhat relieved, but another 45 minutes went by without any word from her. She finally called and said she was lost. I raced over to where she was. All I could do was hold her in my arms. It was 6:30 and had been the longest six hours of my life.

It was hard for me to understand why that six hours had been so devastating to me. It had only been a couple of days before that I was experiencing the thrill of a new relationship. Everything was going fine. I still missed Kathy, but was well on my way to getting over her. Why did I suddenly feel such a need for her? And then, when she did show up and leave again, why did I become so completely overwhelmed by despair that I was ready to kill myself?

After my mind cleared, I was able to look at the situation more objectively. It was God who was at work in this situation. He had given me the great burden to get her back. He had put the sense in me that I could not live without her. In myself, I had already given up on her and she had given up on me. That was why our marriage looked like a hopeless case. Neither one of us cared enough any longer to fight for it. However, God had different plans. He could see what the future held if we remained together. He also knew it would take something drastic before I would really commit myself to Him and to her.

This battle had left me in emotional shambles. I felt ten years older as I reported to work the next day. When my sergeant saw my condition, he said, "Gallagher, I don't know what happened to you, but you're not fit for work. Take a week off!"

He was absolutely right. It was over a week before I would even let Kathy out of my sight. The experience had left me deeply shaken. My independent and self-reliant pride had been shattered. God had finally gotten my attention.

Seven

MY BATTLE WITH SIN

I reported to work a week later, but I definitely was not the same hardhearted, arrogant man I'd been before. My newfound peace of mind dissolved my thirst for action. I had always been aggressive and forceful with inmates and became somewhat confused about how to do my job as a believer.

One day, the Lord convicted me about being a prowler through a passage of Scripture in the first chapter of Proverbs: "My son, if sinners entice you, do not consent.... My son, do not walk in the way with them. Keep your feet from their path, for their feet run to evil, and they hasten to shed blood." That perfectly described the prowler's mentality.

I began asking God to arrange a transfer for me to a new position. My problem was no longer the inmates but my old deputy friends who expected me to continue to respond to situations with violence. The very next day a position became available for the bakery. I applied for it and to my surprise was assigned there.

This got me out of the main population—of inmates and deputies. The bakery was attached to the maximum facility but was basically a world of its own. There were two county bakers working there, along with a team of inmates to help them. As deputy, my primary responsibility was to maintain security and to oversee a crew of inmates who came in after the bakers left to clean up the mess. During my first night working there, I discovered that two of these inmates were Christians. Through some job swapping I was able to fill every position on that crew with believers.

My Christian inmates loved working in the bakery. It gave them an opportunity to fellowship with each other and get out of the stress and noise of the dorms for a while. This was a real blessing to them. I bought testimonial books that they could use to win other inmates to the Lord. *The Cross and the Switchblade*, about David Wilkerson's work among the gangs of New York and Nicky Cruz's story described in *Run, Baby, Run* were my favorites. Since it was against the rules for a deputy to give anything to inmates, I would "smuggle" the books into my group, who, in turn, disseminated them throughout the jail. This probably wasn't the right thing to do, but I was just so excited about the Lord that I *had* to do something there.

My excitement about Christianity was also carried into my marriage. For the first time I began to work on becoming a better husband. However, my wife didn't share those feelings. She explains what she was going through:

> Life with Steve for those first four or five months would prove to be a very difficult period of my life. He was falling in love with me for the first time, but nothing could take away the disgust I felt inside toward him. I could not stand to be near him. I had lost all my respect for him and cringed when he touched me. Many nights I would cry myself to sleep.

I constantly struggled with the temptation to run away. The only reason I stayed was out of the fear of disobeying the Lord.

> *I was suddenly overwhelmed with the temptation to go down to an adult bookstore.*

Steve didn't help his cause either. He was genuinely excited about the Lord, but he was still self-centered and hard to live with. Nevertheless, I hid my true feelings from him because I didn't want to discourage him.

All of this was unknown to me. In my delusion I assumed Kathy was thrilled to have me back now that I was a Christian. My attitude had always been that she was lucky to have me. For the first time, I was beginning to get a small glimpse of the fact that I was fortunate to have her.

Several weeks passed and things were going reasonably well. Kathy and I were getting along better than ever before. Things were calming down for me at the jail, and I was rediscovering the joy of following the Lord.

One morning, as Kathy was at work and I was sitting around the house by myself, I was suddenly overwhelmed with the temptation to go down to an adult bookstore. I hadn't even considered indulging in sexual sin since the six-hour ordeal. The lustful thoughts kept persisting and growing in intensity. It was as if a demonic cloud of sensuality filled the apartment. Memories of things I had done and seen flooded my mind. A feeling of sensuality permeated my being. For years I had lived my life for illicit sexual experiences. Sex had become a deeply rooted idol in my heart, a stronghold of the enemy. Although I was genuinely excited about Christianity, my newfound faith seemed to evaporate in the face of those

> *Sexual sin became a looming mountain in my mind. I could not envision ever being able to scale that lofty peak.*

temptations. They came with such force that my intentions to withstand them simply withered. This was so unexpected and happened so quickly that before I even knew it I was "being carried away" by my own lust. (James 1:14) I went down to the bookstore and gave over to sin.

After it was over, I left in total disgust, stunned by what I'd just done. It was unbelievable that I had walked right back into the old pigpen of perversion. "Lord, I never meant for this to happen," I wailed. I really wanted to live the Christian life. Because it had taken so much to even get me to the point of making that commitment, I had no intention of going back on it. So I couldn't understand how this had happened. I chalked up my failure to the fact that it came so unexpectedly and determined that it would never happen again. Yet, a few days later, the same scenario occurred. My complete inability to fight these urges left me terribly discouraged. Sexual sin became a looming mountain in my mind. I could not envision ever being able to scale that lofty peak but knew that going back was not an option either.

Fear of Kathy leaving me kept me from confessing my failures to her. Things were going well between us, but I knew her commitment to me was still fragile. Something like this could easily send her over the edge; so I dared not let her in on what was going on. This began a double life of secret sin and Christianity that would constitute my life for some time. I would white-knuckle it for a period and then fall flat on my face once again.

One day, a tall black inmate who had been working in our clean up crew told me the Lord had given him a "word" that he should share with me. "The Lord showed me that you will be quitting the Sheriff's Department and going into the ministry as a teacher," he said earnestly. I politely smiled but didn't take it seriously. I had "sweat blood" for that job and had no intention of leaving it. The whole conversation was forgotten within minutes.

The weeks evolved into months as I learned to adjust to being a Christian deputy. My relationship with some of my old friends became strained. They didn't care for the new Deputy Gallagher. They wanted me to be the aggressive officer they had come to admire. I began avoiding their company in favor of deputies who were more laid-back: men I had detested as wimps prior to my return to Christianity.

One evening, I tried sharing the Lord with the guy who had been my best friend. He became angry and told me to leave him alone. It really hurt me and I was upset all that evening. For the first time I entertained thoughts of leaving the department. The next day, I happened to listen to a Chuck Smith message on tape. The subject of his sermon was finding God's will. Since that was what I was contemplating, I became very attentive. During that talk he said, "If you feel God is telling you to do something, then do it and don't look back. Don't let others discourage you from obeying God's call."

By the time I made it to work that day my mind was reeling. I made the long walk back through the jail to the bakery. My clerk was sitting there waiting for me to arrive. After going over our usual business, I shared with him what I felt the Lord was saying to me. "Deputy Gallagher, don't you remember that word of knowledge Smith gave you that day?" Suddenly those words came to mind in full force: "The Lord showed me that you will be quitting the Sheriff's Department and going into the ministry as a teacher."

"Into the ministry!"
They were laughing now.
"How did He call you into
the ministry?"

Now God really had my attention. I spent the rest of that evening praying about it. That night, I came home and shared the whole story with Kathy. "Wow, that's exciting," she responded. We discussed it at length and decided that I should put in my two-week notice and we should plan to move back to Sacramento. My mom's Assembly of God church ran a Bible school I could attend.

I gave my two-week notice the next day. Word quickly got around that I was quitting and immediately several of my old friends confronted me.

"Gallagher, what's this we hear about you quitting?" one of them challenged.

"Yeah, it's true, I am," I responded.

"Why?"

"Because I feel the Lord is calling me into the ministry."

"Into the ministry!" They were laughing now. "How did He call you into the ministry?" they asked incredulously.

"I felt He was speaking to me," I responded lamely.

"Did you hear a voice from heaven or what?" they demanded.

"The Lord has different ways of showing His people what He wants them to do."

They were howling now. "Well, how did He show you?"

"Look, I can't explain it to you. Trust me, I'm doing what He wants."

It went on like this for some time. Finally I was able to break away from them. I went home that night feeling like a complete idiot. Kathy was sympathetic to what I had gone through. She tried to encourage me, "We both felt like God told us this is what we're supposed to do. And besides, don't you remember that Chuck Smith said not to let others talk you out of what you feel God is leading you in?"

Her talk helped, but I still felt confused. That night, as we got in bed, I grabbed my Bible and said a short prayer. "Lord, I really need to hear from You, whether I'm supposed to quit this job and move to Sacramento. Please show me through Your Word." With that, I opened the Bible up randomly and plunked my finger down in Acts 20 where Paul was giving his farewell address to the Ephesian elders. The words stood out clearly to me. "And now, behold, bound in spirit, I am on my way to Jerusalem (Sacramento), not knowing what will happen to me there... But I do not consider my life of any account as dear to myself, in order that I may finish my course, and the ministry which I received from the Lord Jesus, to testify solemnly of the gospel of the grace of God." It was just the confirmation I needed. We were bound for Bible school!

Two weeks later, on February 10, 1983, we headed to Sacramento with our cars crammed full of belongings. As soon as we got into town, I made an appointment with the dean of Trinity Bible School. Pastor Ron Hardin was very gracious to me that day and could sense my zeal. Unfortunately, my arrogance was very evident also. As he shared how I would be studying the various books of the Bible in depth, I impatiently brushed it aside. "I know the Bible pretty good," I stated with the utmost confidence. "I've been listening to Chuck Smith tapes through the whole Bible."

This statement was a revelation of the kind of person they were accepting into their school. I did have a zeal for the Lord, and my academic abilities helped me to do well in school. In fact, I got straight A's that semester. However, there is more to Bible school than scholastic training.

One of the things that really excited me about going to

Bible school was the thought that I would overcome my sexual sin there. Unfortunately, this didn't prove to be the case. Less than a mile from the school were three adult bookstores I had frequented many times in the past. Before long, I began to visit the movie arcades there once again. So I brought this perverted mindset into class and often lusted over the female students.

Needless to say, this was all greatly affecting me in school, although I didn't see the correlation at the time. In spite of the wickedness that filled my heart, I saw myself as better than those around me—even my teachers. My good grades only served to reinforce my delusion. I was full of rebellion and became increasingly critical of my instructors. By the end of the semester in June, I was actually cutting classes and sneaking around smoking cigarettes.

It seemed that summer break couldn't arrive quickly enough. I was sick of the confines of Bible school. Kathy was having her own struggles as well. One night, she suggested we go to a bar. This was the beginnings of another horrible backslide for both of us.

Before long we bought another video recorder and a number of X-rated movies. It didn't take long for me to plumb the depths of sexual sin. Having walked away from my gracious Savior, nothing was now below my dignity. I picked up a swinger's newspaper at an adult bookstore and began scanning the ads about couples that were into swapping partners. I convinced Kathy to join me in the sordid world of swinging. As a result, she became addicted to methamphetamine in an attempt to escape the painful reality of what she was doing.

We stayed backslidden for several months. Kathy finally got sick of the sin and repented. She quickly got on track spiritually. Life became more miserable for me than ever before. It seemed that no matter what I did, I could find no satisfaction. Something would always happen to prevent me from having my way with women. Every situation ended in fail-

Victory was not going to be easily acquired for me, however. I had plunged far from God, and it would not be an easy return.

ure of one kind or another. I somehow knew that God was behind it. One time I even yelled at Him to leave me alone. Gratefully, in His mercy, He didn't honor my request. In the spring of 1984, I gave up. The prodigal son finally came home to his Father. My season of pleasure in sin was just about over.

Victory was not going to be easily acquired for me, however. I had plunged far from God, and it would not be an easy return. When I backslid nine months earlier, I had made an enormously mistaken assumption. "It doesn't really matter what I do because one day I'll just repent and get right with God," I had thought to myself. But in reality every single act of sin had taken me further away from the Lord, and all of that ground would have to be reclaimed one painful step after another. *The Pulpit Commentary* perfectly describes both the agonizing return of the prodigal and the wondrous grace of God that compels him back:

> And they are on the verge of great and awful judgment. If they still go back, it will be "unto perdition;" and if, in God's mercy, they be made to stop ere they have gone to that last length, it will most likely have to be by some sharp scourging process, with many tears, and amid terrible trouble both without and within. What a pitiful journey that must have been when the wretched prodigal resolved at length

It truly was a long and arduous journey back to where I could sense God's presence in my life again.

that he would "arise, and go to his Father"! In what humiliation, fear, shame, distress, he had to urge his weary way along the return road! Only one thing could have been worse — that be should not have come back.

Oh, you who are forsaking Christ, if you be really his, you will have to come back; but no joyous journey will that be for you. No, indeed! It never has been, and never can be. Still blessed be the Lord, who forces you to make it, difficult and hard though it be. It is the hand which was nailed to the cross, and the heart which there was pierced for you, that now wields the scourge which compels you, in sorrow and in shame, to come back to him whom you left.

It truly was a long and arduous journey back to where I could sense God's presence in my life again. I knew when I repented of my despicable actions that the Lord had graciously extended His forgiveness. However, the consequences of having spent nine months in the grossest kind of sin were very extensive. Because of my wicked choices, I had been given over to "degrading passions" and "a depraved mind." (Romans 1:26, 28) I had entered a level of darkness that few come out of.

Just because I made a new commitment to Christ did not nullify the powerful hold that the enemy had on my mind. My thinking had become extremely corrupted with a satanic perspective of sexuality and life. I had lived selfishly for so long that I had very little capacity to think about others, most notably Kathy. I was full of pride, exalting myself one moment and reacting defensively to others the next. My anger and frustration levels were higher than ever before. Words fail me to properly express the price that sin exacted on me and, in turn, on my wife.

To make matters worse, sexual addiction still maintained its vise-like grip on me. Although I began attending church and instituting some positive changes in my life, the temptations to indulge in sexual sin remained as powerful as ever. Not only was this idol still reigning in my heart, but there was no excitement about coming back to the Lord. When I rededicated my life to God in Los Angeles, I was still very vulnerable to sexual temptation, but I was excited about the things of God. Now, there was nothing but dry drudgery.

Nevertheless, in some unknown way, there was a resolve deep within me that I had had enough. I had indulged nearly every sick fantasy I had ever entertained. The message could not have been clearer that sin does not satisfy. In spite of this growing conviction, I continued to return to the same pigsty time and again.

One of our first priorities was to move away from the house we had lived in during this wretched period of our lives. An opportunity presented itself to fulfill my lifelong dream of living in the country. We were able to purchase a little farm on a lease option not too far from town.

Moving out to the country helped me to refocus my priorities. It also kept me further away from the areas of temptation. The Lord quietly helped me to see that I needed to institute certain disciplines into my life.

First of all, Kathy and I both began to spend time in prayer and Bible study every morning. This was very difficult at first, but I was becoming increasingly determined to get my life right with God. We would force ourselves to spend twenty minutes in prayer and a half an hour in Bible study. In addition to this, my outside sales position made it possible to listen to Christian radio for several hours every day.

In the meantime, Kathy helped me by keeping me accountable with money. She gave me a small allotment for food and gas but kept a tight rein on the finances. I simply didn't have the money to spend on pornography and sexual sin. She also made me answerable for my actions by staying in contact with me throughout the day. At night, she was not afraid to ask me how I was doing. Her involvement with my struggle made all the difference in the world. She loved me and was not willing to lose me to sexual sin.

Another thing the Lord began dealing with me about was watching television. Every evening I would plop down in front of the TV and watch old reruns. I resisted His promptings until I read Dave Wilkerson's book, *Set The Trumpet To Thy Mouth*, in which he discusses the effects television has on the believer. I finally repented and got rid of the television. I didn't realize until later the detrimental effect it was having on my walk with God.

The Lord also confronted me about a close friendship I retained. Mark tolerated my Christianity but had no interest in the Lord himself. I wouldn't get involved with his party lifestyle, but we would still occasionally hang out together. Kathy started to notice that a change would come over me when I was around him and convinced me that I needed to break ties. I knew she was right, but it was very difficult. He had been one of the few people in my entire life that had accepted me for who I was. One day, I told him I had to end our friendship. He didn't understand and accused me of being self-righteous. I couldn't explain it to his satisfaction, but I had to follow through with my decision.

There was one more important thing that needed to

change: my selfishness in bed. In my macho mentality, I thought that the kitchen was for the wife and the bedroom was for the man. One day, the Lord

> *That was the last time I was ever unfaithful to my wife. Sexual sin had finally lost its grip on my life!*

helped me to see that she also had needs and desires. I made a commitment to begin considering her needs before my own in our times of intimacy. As I started putting my wife first, I started to experience a sense of fulfillment in our lovemaking that my fantasies could never provide. It was amazing.

Meanwhile, the temptations to commit sexual sin were not coming my way nearly as often or with the same degree of force. Sometimes I gave in, but as time went by I was increasingly denying them. Spending time with the Lord every day was building spiritual strength within me that had never been there previously. Something was changing inside me. I occasionally had lustful thoughts, but they weren't overpowering like they had once been. I was busy doing my job and simply trying to live like a Christian.

Then one day in May of 1985, I was driving through town and got tempted to visit an adult bookstore. I foolishly gave in to the urge and viewed some movies. This sent me into another spiritual tailspin. I binged on sex for the next two weeks, culminating in a visit to a massage parlor. It was a very unsatisfying encounter, and I left the place absolutely disgusted with myself and fed up with paying the penalty for empty, unfulfilling experiences. "Sex with my wife is better than this!" I told myself. That was the last time I was ever unfaithful to my wife. Sexual sin had finally lost its grip on my life!

Kathy had been unbelievably patient with me. She was

determined to stay on course with the Lord regardless of what I did. She watched me with cautious optimism. After several months, it became obvious that something was different about me. She actually began to respect me and look up to me as the spiritual leader of the home. Her love for me had been growing, and now there was nothing to stop it.

In September of 1985—four months after my visit to that massage parlor—she flew to her company's headquarters in Cleveland, Ohio for a month of further training. This was a major test for me. I had complete freedom and had to deal with some real temptations, but I managed to stand strong and resist them.

Having made it through this trial, we both sensed that God was opening the door for me to return to Bible school—if that was what we wanted.

Now we had another major decision to make. We could either live the comfortable Christian life on the little farm the Lord had blessed us with, or we could give it up for an unknown future in ministry.

Eight

PURE LIFE MINISTRIES

*A*n unshakeable call of God was still on my life that I could not deny. There was another Assembly of God two-year Bible school located in Sacramento. It was part of Capital Christian Center, a church with a congregation of over five thousand members. Glen Cole, one of the thirteen executive presbyters of the denomination, was the senior pastor. My application was accepted and I entered Capital Bible Institute in December of 1985.

Attending an A/G school put me in a dilemma because of their rule forbidding the credentialing of those who had been divorced and remarried.* I had no idea what I would do once I graduated school. However, over a period of three months, I sensed the Lord directing me into the field of counseling and addiction recovery. I attended a meeting for alcoholics and drug abusers, and the thought occurred to me to start a group for *sexual* addicts—a concept almost completely unheard of in those days.

This idea gained strength in my mind over the coming

---

* This rule has since been changed.

> *Every day I received new confirmation that starting this ministry was God's will.*

days. Every pastor I sought counsel from thought it was a potentially powerful undertaking. There were a number of ministries that were reaching out to homosexuals in different cities, but nobody was offering help to sexual addicts in general at that time.

Every day I received new confirmation that starting this ministry was God's will. I had to come up with a name, of course. Several possibilities came to mind: Back to Decency Ministry, Life of Liberty Ministry, New Liberty Ministry, and New Purity Ministry. However, none of them set right with me. As I continued to think about it, I finally came up with the right one: Pure Life Ministries! On April 26, 1986 Kathy and I applied for a fictitious business name, opened a checking account and got a post office box. We were in business!

In the meantime, I received a call from a producer of *The 700 Club*. I had sent them our testimony several months prior to this but never expected to hear from them. That spring they sent a reporter and film crew to California to tape a re-enactment of our story.

Another important thing was occurring for me at that time. For a brief two-year period—coinciding with my attendance—Nels and Juanita Hinman oversaw the counseling department at our church and taught all of the counseling classes in our school. They were not psychotherapists; they were biblical counselors. Everything they taught about counseling was rooted in Scripture.

I would sit in Nels' classes spellbound by his ability to share the Word of God in such a simple and practical manner. No matter what problem was discussed in class, he always had an answer from Scripture. I had heard many theories about helping people with their problems, but there was no doubt in my mind that what was being presented was truth.

In spite of that conviction, I still was fairly convinced that the really difficult problems needed "professional" help. Why I still believed this is a mystery, considering the fact that not one psychologist I had ever visited had offered any real help. Nevertheless, it was difficult to shake the idea that they were the "experts" and the only ones qualified to handle tough situations.

However, over time this thinking changed as I realized that the Word of God really *does* have the answers to people's problems. God had created people to live a certain way and when they got off course in some aspect of life they inevitably experience problems. Although the troubles were sometimes complicated or difficult, the basic solutions were simple in that they could be found in one's relationship to God.

When Nels heard about Pure Life Ministries, he invited me to be a guest on his enormously successful local radio talk show. I received a number of calls from struggling men who heard me on the program, and we began a support group in our apartment the following Tuesday evening.

After we had our first meeting, I went on a three-day bread and water fast in the mountains. I spent many hours praying about this new ministry and also about sexual lust, which continued to plague me. One day, the Lord made it very real to me that Pure Life Ministries would eventually have a national scope. In my excitement I shared this with a number of people close to me, but nobody—including Kathy—took me seriously. This was due to my level of immaturity and impulsive nature.

1986 proved to be an incredibly demanding year. Since I was a student and was no longer working, I was able to

> *The word about Pure Life was gradually getting out in the Christian community of Northern California.*

cover our rent by managing the apartment complex where we lived. Besides attending school full time and managing our apartments, I also returned to junior college to take the two classes I needed to complete my associate's degree in Social Sciences. On top of all of this, I was busy writing the first edition of *At the Altar of Sexual Idolatry*, a book describing sexual addiction and the steps out of it. In addition to that, I was also busy doing all of the legal work to apply for tax-exempt status, talking to various pastors and, of course, holding the meetings. These were very difficult and yet exciting days for us.

During the next several months, I appeared on various local Christian radio and television stations. The word about Pure Life was gradually getting out in the Christian community of Northern California. We had since outgrown our living room and moved the meeting into the church. A reporter from *The Sacramento Bee* interviewed me, and the article appeared in the newspaper a few days later.

Unbeknownst to me, God was seriously dealing with a man named Richard Simpson. Richard's sex life had been terribly out of control since he had been involved in orgies with friends in school. His whole life was lived for sexual gratification. For years he and his wife Rebecca had been mixed up in swinging. She thought her involvement in his seedy lifestyle would help their marriage, but things only got worse. Eventually she became a born again Christian, but Richard had no intention of quitting his lifestyle.

One evening, as Rebecca was reading her Bible in bed, Richard thrust a pornographic magazine into her face and exclaimed, "This is my god!" She considered divorcing him, but God clearly led her to stick it out with him. Rebecca continued to pray for him.

One evening, Richard was sitting in a bathhouse. There was sex going on all around him, but he felt empty and miserable. He went into his private room and dropped to his knees and cried out to God to set him free. The next day he went to Rebecca's pastor and confessed his struggles. The minister didn't know what to tell him but prayed that God would provide an answer.

That answer appeared on a page of *The Sacramento Bee* the next day! He started attending our meetings and before long, they were both completely involved in the ministry. Richard came to the meetings, and Rebecca helped Kathy minister to the men's wives. They were a wonderful support to us for a long time while we were in California. Richard later quit his job in management with a telephone company and today pastors a church in Northern California.

Others were helped in those early days as well. Ron and Omera Jenkins seemed to be an ordinary, Christian couple. He was an accountant and she was an office worker. However, Ron had been entertaining homosexual fantasies for many years. Although he had grown up in church and had never acted on those temptations, they persisted.

Eventually he gave in to his impulses and left Omera to live with another man. She was extremely upset and didn't know what to do. It was then she heard about the group of sexual addicts and their wives' meeting at Capital Christian Center. Friends were giving her all kinds of advice. She was confused when she showed up at the wives' meeting. Rebecca shared with her what had happened in her marriage. She encouraged Omera to take it to God in prayer.

Refusing to idly sit by while her husband threw his life away in homosexuality, Omera spent the next several weeks fasting and praying for him. One night, Ron showed up as suddenly as he had left. The two of them began coming to the meetings together until Ron was strong enough to stand on his own again. Both Omera and Rebecca were beautiful examples of God's selfless love for the sinner. In the meantime, our group—comprising struggling men and their hurting wives—averaged 40 people per meeting.

In November 1986 I graduated Bible school. Two days after the ceremony a special speaker came to our church on a Sunday evening. During that service, the Lord spoke very clearly to my heart that He wanted me to double my devotional time to two hours. I started driving to the church at 6:00 a.m. every morning and would spend two or three hours seeking the Lord. This was a glorious time for me. I would walk through the pews, up around the balcony and back and forth at the altar. Sometimes God's presence seemed to hover powerfully in the sanctuary.

Not long after this I decided to go on a five-day fast at a Christian camp on the coast of Northern California. Because of low blood sugar, I was sick most of the time I was there. Nevertheless, I spent many hours in prayer and God really came to me. I left there feeling as though He was about to do something big—I just didn't know what.

When I arrived home, I began adding fresh material to *At the Altar of Sexual Idolatry*, hoping to provide more complete answers in the book. The next few days were remarkable. As I sat typing on the computer, it seemed as though my fingers were being driven by another source. I was typing truths I simply didn't have knowledge of yet! God's hand was clearly on that book.

A couple of months later, Don Wildmon came to Sacramento to speak in a special rally hosted by a local pro-decency group I had become involved with. I was given the task of picking Don up at his motel room and took the opportunity to share with him about Pure Life Ministries. He invited me to write an article about my work and to submit it to his monthly magazine, *The AFA Journal*.

> *In January 1988, an even bigger break came my way when a producer from "The Oprah Winfrey Show" called and invited me on the program.*

One morning, during my drive to the church, I felt God telling me to have a toll-free line installed in our apartment because I would be receiving calls from across the nation. I didn't know anything about "800 lines" but obeyed nonetheless. In the meantime, a friend and I drove to Atlanta, appearing on radio shows in different cities along the way. While we were gone, the article in *The AFA Journal* came out. That month over 900 phone calls came into our new toll-free line! Suddenly, my claims of having a national calling didn't seem so far-fetched.

This was the "break" I had been waiting for. I worked feverishly to respond to all of the inquiries and to promote the ministry in other ways. I was consumed with taking Pure Life into the "big time." Nels Hinman tried to caution me not to get ahead of the Lord. He said that God had a plan for me and that I should make my relationship to Him my primary focus and let Him worry about the promotion of the ministry. I wanted to be close to the Lord, but I was also very ambitious.

In January 1988, an even bigger break came my way when a producer from *The Oprah Winfrey Show* called and invited me on the program. I was flown to Chicago and put up in the Hilton Hotel. Being too nervous to sleep, I spent the night in prayer. The Lord helped me to give a clear-cut testimony of what Jesus had done in my life. In fact, at one point during the show, when I expressed my love for Kathy, the entire (mostly female) audience stood up and cheered!

This exposure opened the door for me to appear on a number of national Christian programs as well. Not long after I was on *The Oprah Winfrey Show* the story broke about Jim Bakker's fall into sexual sin. Since I was virtually the only one talking about sexual addiction in the Church in those days, I was able to appear on radio and TV shows across the nation. Everything seemed to be going just the way I had hoped.

I would sometimes claim to those around me that I had a great burden for people that drove me on so relentlessly. The truth is that I was a work-a-holic full of self-ambition. I honestly did want to help people, but I definitely had mixed motives. There was a lot of self in everything I did. Ministry became a vehicle to fulfill a very deep-seated desire to be recognized as someone important.

I was once again reading biographies about ministers and missionaries who were used by God in a great way. Reading these stories kept me motivated to pray and to live a godly life, but they also deepened my determination to do everything within my power to make Pure Life Ministries a "great work of God."

I had been given a vision of what my life work would be in much the same way the biblical character Joseph had. What I didn't realize at the time was that—just like Joseph's vision was put to death in an Egyptian prison—mine too was about to suffer a tremendous blow.

Nine

KENTUCKY

s word spread about Pure Life Ministries, we decided to go on a speaking tour across the nation and began booking services in churches throughout the South and then up the East Coast. Kathy loved her job with the insurance company she had worked at for five years but was willing to give it up to go with me.

Although we were planning to return to Sacramento after our nine-month tour, we felt led to sell or give away nearly everything we owned. One night, I came home and discovered that someone had bought an antique bed that had meant a lot to me. I panicked inside. "What have I done!?" I asked myself. Just then, I heard the same voice which had spoken to me in Los Angeles: "Birds have nests and foxes have holes in the ground but the Son of man hath nowhere to lay His head." It was just the reassurance I needed.

We bought an old 21-foot motor home and, in January 1989, set out on our trip. I spoke at Bible schools, did radio shows and preached at various churches. Everywhere we went I shared my testimony of how God had set me free from sexual sin. Whenever Kathy and I arrived in a city we were scheduled to minister in, we would find a K-Mart parking lot where we could park for the week. It was also important that there was a gas station with a clean bathroom located nearby, since the R.V. toilet was essentially unusable.

Living like this was difficult enough, but then one thing after another began to go wrong with the motor home. First, the hot water heater started malfunctioning intermittently. There were times when one of us would be taking a shower and the water would abruptly turn ice-cold. While that person stood soaped up and shivering, the other would have to go outside and try to re-light the pilot light again—sometimes in the midst of a driving rainstorm! Next, the refrigerator quit working, and we had to use an ice chest. Then the microwave, the heater in the cab and the stereo all quit working. My frustration and anger over these difficulties made life even more unbearable for Kathy.

Shortly after we left Sacramento, the producers of *The 700 Club* invited me to appear on the show again. After Pat Robertson interviewed me, the ministry chaplain asked me to speak to the CBN staff at their weekly chapel service. In the twenty minutes I had, I shared a brief testimony and then preached my heart out. As I concluded, I asked those to stand who wanted to forsake any habitual sin and make a new commitment to Christ. Amazingly, half of the audience stood up. Some people were openly crying. Even though I was still a very immature Christian, the Lord used my testimony to affect lives.

In the meantime, we found out that the couple we had left in charge of the ministry was no longer taking care of business. They weren't returning phone calls or fulfilling orders that were coming in. We couldn't return since we had nine months of services booked in churches across the country. Because of this and through a number of different circumstances, we sensed the Lord directing us to move into the Cincinnati area. The more we prayed about it, the more certain we were that it was God's will for us to relocate the ministry there.

As March approached, we began to ask the Lord to provide us a piece of property that could be used both as a house and a ministry headquarters.

When we originally planned out our tour, we tried to book services in Florida during the first two weekends of March. However, despite all our efforts, we couldn't get one single church to have us. This left two weeks open for us in the midst of a tight schedule. Now we understood why. God was orchestrating everything.

As March approached, we began to ask the Lord to provide us a piece of property that could be used both as a house and a ministry headquarters. During our daily prayer times, we prayed for the place *we knew* He was going to supply for us.

Since we weren't spending money at restaurants and motels, we were able to put aside most of the offerings we received from my speaking engagements. By the time we arrived in Cincinnati, we had accumulated nearly $3,000 to put toward the purchase of a place.

When we got into town, we went straight to a Christian real estate agent who had been referred to us. I explained our situation to him, and he said he would get back to us. We waited and waited. I called him, but it quickly became obvious he was giving us the run-around. As an ex-agent, I could guess what he was thinking. "These people don't have a fixed income. The ministry has no assets or credit, and there isn't a bank around that will loan them money. They're obviously a waste of time."

However, we knew God was going to do something; so we went out looking for property ourselves. After about a week, we had exhausted every possibility around Cincinnati, so we began searching in northern Kentucky.

We found a doublewide mobile home on five acres for sale, ignoring the fact that the property was very steep and had no possibility for future expansion. I worked out a verbal deal with the owner, only to find out a few days later that he had changed his mind. We were devastated. We were so certain that God had led us to Kentucky, but now we were running out of time. I was beginning to think that we had imagined the entire thing. But Kathy was undaunted. "We're not giving up!" she exclaimed. "We're going to find another place!" I agreed, but all the enthusiasm had drained out of me.

We visited another real estate office, but the agent quickly lost interest when he realized we couldn't qualify for a new loan. He pawned us off on a part-time agent who was happy to have any business. She was inexperienced and didn't realize what poor prospects we were. She began searching through her Multiple Listing book and came across a mobile home on a half of an acre. "We're not interested in that place. God stopped us from getting that other place so He could give us something better!" I confidently asserted. I felt that if the Lord stopped us from purchasing a mobile home on five acres, He certainly wasn't going to have us turn around and buy one on less than one acre. The lady didn't look convinced.

We went through page after page of that book. Every time we found something of interest, she would call the listing agent only to discover that the people weren't interested in loaning the money themselves. We finally got down to the last page in the book. And there it was: a little house on twelve acres owned by a local broker.

As soon as we pulled into the driveway, I knew it was the right place. The roof sagged and the house badly needed paint, but the

"And Lord, we want You to know this is Your property and You do with it as You see fit. We give it to You."

view of the green hills of Kentucky was spectacular! We immediately drove to the broker's office and worked out the deal. Now all we had to do was come up with another $7,000 within the next two months. We headed to our next speaking engagement in Atlanta, excited about how God was going to provide.

During the following two months, Kathy and I went from church to church as we made our way up the Atlantic seaboard. When we returned on May 15th, we had just enough for the down payment. We had two wicker chairs with which to furnish our new home. That evening, after we made ourselves a makeshift bed on the floor, we sat down in those two chairs and said a long prayer of gratitude to the Lord. "And Lord," I concluded, "We want You to know this is Your property and You do with it as You see fit. We give it to You." We had no idea of how He would take us up on that later!

For the next several months we drove back and forth to various churches, ministering on weekends and returning to Kentucky during the week. We changed our address and phone number, and the ministry was back in operation. The highlight of every day was to go to the post office in the hopes that some money—any money—might arrive. In those days a $20-gift was a thrill! Each month, we received just enough to pay the mortgage and utilities, with precious little left over.

Meanwhile, Kathy and I were once again having real

marital problems. Actually they had resurfaced during the tour across the country. I kept taking out my frustrations on her. Things were temporarily better when we first moved into the house. However, it wasn't long before my anger began to rear its ugly head again. Kathy felt as though she had to walk on eggshells around me. I was also very demanding and greatly lacked appreciation for her.

One day, I made a cutting comment to her and she blew up. I realized I was wrong and apologized. She would usually warm right up to me when I admitted fault, but this time she didn't respond that way. When I told her that I loved her, she exploded. "Don't tell me you love me!" she yelled. "You don't love me. If you loved me you would act like you did!" Her comments stung, but they also affected me very deeply. She tells about this episode:

Steve was much easier to live with at this point than early on in our relationship. He wasn't mean like he had once been. However, he was still very frustrated. This was tolerable for me when we were still in California, but when we were forced to be with each other continually, his difficult nature simply became too much. One day, I snapped and told him that he didn't love me.

I think for the first time he really comprehended how he was treating me. From then on he began to show more patience and kindness. It was definitely another turning point in our marriage.

When I began treating Kathy with more gentleness and love, she started to blossom as a person. Her defensiveness and rebellion gradually gave way to a joy that I had never seen in her before. The more love I showed her, the more she came out of her shell. Her "new" personality, in turn, was a great encouragement to me. Instead of working against each other, we began working as a team.

Actually, Kathy was the one who taught me how to love. I had grown up in a home where warmth was never displayed. Each member of our family remained distant from the others. My father's selfishness dominated the home to the point that even my mother didn't feel comfortable expressing affection. I simply had no comprehension about what marital love was like. Kathy had learned about it by watching the way her parents treated each other. She taught me that we were not two separate people living together— the mentality I brought into the marriage—but that we were "one flesh." (Genesis 2:24) Therefore, she wanted to be involved with everything that went on with me. It wasn't out of nosiness or from being insecure about my faithfulness. She simply loved me and was absorbed in every phase of my life. To Kathy, love equated with interest. I gradually began to reciprocate this kind of attention and affection.

> *She taught me that we were not two separate people living together—the mentality I brought into the marriage—but that we were "one flesh."*

In the meantime, people continued to call seeking advice about their struggles with sexual sin. I would repeatedly tell different individuals what they needed to do. Having my book *At the Altar of Sexual Idolatry* available for them was a big help, since the pathway to freedom was laid out for readers to follow. However, as I talked to men over the phone, it became evident early on that they were not implementing the principles outlined in the book into their lives. Sexual sin had such a hold on them that most of them felt as though they didn't have a "fighting chance." I knew from my own experience how hard it is for a man to fight this battle by himself.

One day, the thought came to me that struggling men needed a place where they could go to receive daily hands-on help. Although I knew it would be far more effective than what I was offering them at that point, this was not what I desired to do. I wanted to continue preaching and appearing on radio shows. Nevertheless, the idea persisted to the point that it became obvious that it was God's will. Following His lead, we began making plans to open our home to struggling men. We announced in our ministry newsletter that the program would commence on January 1, 1990. Six men responded and committed to coming.

While this was going on, God was also working in the hearts of Kathy's parents. Mel and Shirley strongly believed the Lord wanted them to move to Kentucky to help us. They sold everything they owned—thirty years worth of possessions—and arrived in November. They immediately bought a mobile home. With the men due to arrive in January, we had to get it set up on the property quickly.

December of 1989 was the coldest December anyone could remember in a long time. The average temperature that month was nineteen degrees, with many days not rising above five degrees. Because we were so poor, we had to do much of the work of setting up the mobile home ourselves. One thing after another went wrong. For instance, our water lines froze and busted, after we had already backfilled the entire hundred feet of trench. With the temperature hovering around zero, we had to dig out the frozen dirt with a shovel to replace the broken pipes. Eventually our mission was accomplished.

The men arrived during the first week of 1990 right on schedule. Little did I know that I was in way over my head. First of all, I was far too busy. Just about every weekend Kathy and I

All of this gave the men the impression that we didn't know what we were doing—and in many ways we didn't!

had to travel to churches in neighboring states. During the week I had to answer phone calls, fill orders for teaching materials, do the maintenance on the houses, and answer mail. We had an accountability meeting on Tuesday evening and a Bible study on Thursday night. On top of all of that, I had to counsel each man individually.

Perhaps the aspect of the program that made things the most difficult for everyone was simply the lack of professionalism. The men's home was just an old farmhouse. The "staff" consisted of Kathy and myself. Furthermore, there was no real structure to this "mom and pop" operation. All of this gave the men the impression that we didn't know what we were doing—and in many ways we didn't!

Since we ate together, had meetings together, lived together—indeed, did almost everything together—the guys became too familiar with us. Any respect they might have had for us quickly vanished. When I would attempt to correct or even discipline one of them, he would immediately rebel against my leadership.

On top of all of that was the problem of Steve Gallagher. Although I had changed a great deal since becoming a Christian, I was still very much full of myself. Serious-minded to the point of being fretful and frustrated, my countenance was anything but gracious. Although people often misunderstood me, there was no getting around the fact that I could also be defensive, impatient, abrasive and short-tempered. At times in counseling I was too demanding and intolerant. It was as if I were reverting back to my days of dealing with inmates in the jail. In a nutshell, I was not very Christ-like.

Over the months that followed, my relationship with the men became increasingly strained. There is no question that they were a difficult group of guys to deal with, but my spiritual immaturity caused the situation to escalate into hostility. One day in June 1990, everybody left with the exception of one guy. Then Mel and Shirley decided to return to California to be with their other children and grandchildren. Although their life savings had been sunk into the mobile home, they donated it to the ministry.

I blamed myself for everything that went wrong. I was simply a difficult person to be around—let alone live with—and sank under an overwhelming sense of guilt and condemnation. I became depressed, feeling hopeless that my harsh nature would ever change.

In all fairness, I was only part of the difficulty. It was a new program, and these problems were to be expected, especially in a challenging ministry like this. Furthermore, these men were extremely troubled, having spent years giving themselves over to self-indulgence and self-gratification. Whereas I had occasional lapses in my walk with God, they completely lived in the flesh. I had a brash nature, but at least I was striving to please the Lord with my life. These men lived for themselves and had little concern about others. Their selfishness manifested itself in rebellion, criticism, and anger.

For instance, Kevin, an aging hippie from Boston, would occasionally go into demonic rages. One day, he became so angry with me that he screamed at the top of his voice, "Steve Gallagher, I hate you! I hate God! Satan, I worship you!" It was little wonder that they collectively rose up in pride against the correction they were receiving.

Nevertheless, knowing this was of little comfort to me. The only thing that stood out to me was how unmerciful and unloving I was. I began to cry out to God in the

A lifetime of being rejected by others because of my abrasive personality troubled me deeply.

most heart-felt anguish imaginable. A lifetime of being rejected by others because of my abrasive personality troubled me deeply. My abrasive nature had always kept people at arm's length, but now I had to live with people—and love them! I had never had natural warmth as a person and couldn't manufacture it. The only thing for me to do was plead with the Lord to change me, to make me more like Jesus. In spite of my total dejection and despair, the conviction that I must continue the live-in program remained unshakeable. We had to go on despite my inner struggles.

Lance was the one man who didn't take part in the mass exodus. He was a professional pianist who had once played for a nationally acclaimed ballet company. He had even performed for President and Mrs. Reagan at the Kennedy Center! Unfortunately, homosexuality and drug abuse had hollowed out his life of all meaning. Eventually, he became a Christian, but he still could not seem to get the victory over his sexual sin. He heard me on a radio show one day and soon after entered the live-in program.

When he arrived at Pure Life, he soon discovered that he still had tons of baggage stashed deep within the crevices of his heart. Years of self-pity had stockpiled, along with deep fears, resentments, arrogance, worldly wisdom and sophistication. As these layers of selfishness were exposed, there were many times he wanted to leave.

Gradually, God began to do a work in his heart as he accumulated days, weeks, and months of freedom from sexual sin.

As God revealed the ugliness of his heart, he started looking at the faults of those around him in an attempt to make himself feel or look better. Most of the time he was a very pleasant person to talk to. Nevertheless, beneath the surface Lance was very arrogant. His haughtiness displayed itself as a quiet smugness of superiority, having a disdain for anyone who was not on his intellectual level. He was just as critical of Kathy and me as those who left, but when it came right down to it, he knew he had to stay.

Gradually, God began to do a work in his heart as he accumulated days, weeks, and months of freedom from sexual sin. He had a great determination to know the Bible and learn about the things of God. In the meantime, the Lord brought in other guys who were committed to enduring, and the program started to come together.

Eventually, Lance graduated the live-in program and was invited to come on staff. It was not long before he became the primary counselor for the men. He spent his days studying the principles of biblical counseling and his evenings in the actual practice of it. The early days were rough, but over time God really developed him into a first-rate counselor.

Soon after Lance took over the live-in counseling, a young guy named Tim contacted us from a state mental hospital in New York City. Tim was desperate and in a crisis situation. His most immediate problem was his complete inability to stop exposing himself to women. He was so out of control that, as soon as the psychiatrist would release him from his "locked down" room, Tim would undress at the nearest window and display his "birthday suit" to the city of New York! Even the increase of medication, doubling it from two dosages of Thorazine to four (hence the name, "the Thorazine shuffle"), did not deter him. Tim's sexual addiction had driven him to insanity. Divine intervention was his only hope.

We felt that this young man was too far gone to be helped at Pure Life. Not only that, he did not even have a relationship with the Lord. And yet, every time we tried to dismiss the idea, it seemed as though God kept prodding us to accept him. So, against our better judgment, this unsaved mental patient was accepted into the live-in program during the winter of 1991.

Tim really took to the program, accepting the Lord soon after arriving. The Word of God was fresh to him, and he had the spiritual innocence of a little child. Nevertheless, he also had a lot of problems. He was very confused, easily upset and constantly thinking about sex. At one of the first meetings he attended at Pure Life, he got so angry with one of the other men that he left the meeting, running across a field in the pouring rain, crying and screaming at the top of his lungs. Despite his deep-seated troubles, Tim seemed to have a genuine hunger to know God. He was very difficult in those early days, but as he spent time in prayer and in the Scriptures, a gradual change began to take place within him. As he was forced—for the first time in his life—to take responsibility for his own actions, he started to experience genuine repentance. With this turning away from sin and toward God came an overwhelming sense of hope that he could truly change. Jesus Christ became a reality for him.

Upon graduating from the program, he too was asked to become a counselor in the live-in program. This arrangement went on happily for several months.

Photo Album

Passport photo of Frances Gallagher, with Steve and his sister Kathy in 1960, just before moving to England for two years.

Don't be fooled by the sweet look in this little boy's face. He was well on his way to becoming a little hellion!

Steve at age 19, just before entering college. In the background is the house in Sacramento where he grew up. His bedroom, facing the street, was the scene of much drug abuse and promiscuity. Steve was sitting in his car here when the old gang approached him two years prior to this picture.

Steve's early
life revolved
around adult
bookstores,
massage parlors
and strip clubs.

Steve's driver's license
obtained after Stephanie
left him in 1977.

Kathy, about a year
after the marriage.
She looks happy,
but she was hanging
on for dear life.

Wedding picture taken with the parents of the groom in January 1980. This occurred ten years after Steve came to the Lord and ten years (almost to the day) before he and Kathy began the live-in program.

Mel and Shirley Irwin, Kathy's parents. They became very angry with Steve when they found out about his secret life of perversion. However, when he repented, they were quick to forgive and forget, and were a source of strength and stability to Steve and Kathy as they returned to the Lord.

Graduation from the LASD Academy in 1981.
Steve poses with his oldest sister Jeannette
and Sheriff Peter J. Pitchess.

A smug deputy with
off-duty revolver.
The smile barely masks
the fact that he was
full of fear, anger
and perversion: a time
bomb waiting to go off.

Capital Christian Center in Sacramento. After a long
struggle with sexual sin, Steve finally got the victory
and entered the Bible school located at this church.

While at Capital Christian Center, Steve and Kathy
founded Pure Life Ministries. Some men pray together
during a support group meeting held at the church in 1987.

A producer interviews the Gallaghers in 1986
for *The 700 Club*. Sexual addiction was a concept
almost unheard of when Steve shared with the
viewers how God had set him free.

The house in Kentucky that the Gallaghers purchased
in 1989. The Pure Life live-in program began with six
men in this little house in January 1990. By the end
of the next year there would be 17 men crammed into it!

Kathy in a light-hearted moment. "There is no question that Kathy Irwin was God's choice for my life," the author states. "She has been easy-going enough to handle my intense personality and yet serious about her walk with God. What more could I have asked for?"

The Fairview Home, where hundreds of men have found freedom from habitual sexual sin. Almost immediately the Pure Life team added a 2,000 sq. ft. dormitory to the back of it.

In early 1992, the staff
watched a videotape of Hong Kong
missionary Jackie Pullinger
speaking at a conference. Steve
would later say that watching
this woman speak one time had
more of an effect on his life
than hundreds of hours of
listening to radio preachers.
Jackie spoke at the
*2003 Purity and Intimacy
Conference* held by PLM.

In 1995, Steve and
David Leopold, a Faith
Home minister, spent
a month bumming around
Turkey and Greece,
visiting the ancient
ruins of New Testament
cities. Here the two
pose with a family
they stayed with in
modern-day Lystra.

The Guest House, one
of the Faith Homes.
Doug and Millie were
house parents here.
The Gallaghers stayed
in this home many
times through the
years.

Early picture of Rex Andrews (on the left with guitar) with three early Pentecostal ministers. John G. Lake is seated fourth from the left.

Although Steve and Kathy never knew Rex Andrews personally, he had an enormous effect on their lives. He spent nearly all night every night interceding for others during the final 30 years of his life. Here he sits with Bible open in the Faith Homes during the '50s. He died in 1973.

Steve and Kathy with Doug and Millie in a recent picture.
Mr. Andrews poured himself into the lives of Doug and Millie.
The impact he had on them is largely responsible for their
earnest love for God and others and their rich insights
into the Kingdom of God.

Millie in a conversation with Jimmy Jack
at the *2003 Purity & Intimacy Conference.*
Both are board members of Pure Life Ministries.

Doug praying next to David Ravenhill at the *2003 Purity & Intimacy Conference*. Another man who greatly affected Doug's life was David's father, Leonard Ravenhill.

Evangelists Glenn and Jessie Meldrum became close friends of the Gallaghers at Brownsville in 1997. Glenn stirs the hearts of congregations with his passionate cry for holiness.

Jeff and Rose Colón, faithful friends and godly ministers. These two have given their best years living out God's mercy to struggling men and hurting wives.

Justin Carabello, George Mooney, John Delmon and Bradley Furges have each become an integral part of what God is doing at Pure Life Ministries. Each one of them is a living testimony to the fact that God can save and transform the most hopeless sinner.

The Pure Life chapel under construction in 2000.
Building projects have been a constant aspect
of ministry since we moved to Fairview.

A meeting at the PLM chapel. Some meetings are so full
of the presence of God that nobody wants to leave at
the end of the meeting.

Steve and Linda Frakes run a Bible correspondence school under the auspices of Mt. Zion Ministries in Pensacola, Florida. Because of their efforts, approximately 15,000 copies of *At the Altar of Sexual Idolatry* have been sent free of charge to inmates in 2,200 institutions. Their story was featured in *Break Free: from the Lusts of this World*.

Jim and Lenora Woodall were missionaries to Nicaragua for a number of years before Jim became the CEO of Concerned Women for America. Jim is a PLM board member.

Two men graduating from the PLM live-in program.
Six to nine months of intense, spiritual discipleship
has gone into each man by the time he graduates.
These men are being sent back home prepared to live
victoriously in a sexualized culture.

The vast hayfield known as "The Ridge" has been
the site of many special encounters with God. Apart
from it being the place where God revealed His mercy
to Steve, most of the men who graduate the live-in
program take precious memories with them of time
spent alone with God on these rolling hills.

Steve and Jeff in Cali, Colombia in 2003. In the foreground
are Ruth Ruibal and her daughters, Abby and Sarai. The story
of the martyrdom of Ruth's husband Julio was made famous
in the first *Transformations* video. Ruth has become a dear
friend of Steve and Kathy's.

The new Pure Life Ministries Headquarters building in
Dry Ridge, KY. The staff felt led to pray for the purchase
of this building in 2002. $40,000 was needed within two months
to close the deal. God laid it on Steve's heart to believe Him
for $600 a day above the normal ministry needs. Just enough
money came in to close the deal on time.

Ten

AN EXPANDING WORK

*L*ittle by little things started to come together for Pure Life Ministries. Lance handled the bulk of the counseling for the live-in program. He received help from a dramatically matured Tim. We also hired a graduate to handle the maintenance of the ministry buildings and vehicles. Another guy filled the orders that continued to flow in for my books and tapes.

However, one of the problems we continued to face was what to do with the men who for one reason or another couldn't come to the live-in program. We wanted to do more to help them as well. So we decided to develop a new program that they could go through from home which became known as The Overcomers-At-Home Program. We announced it in our newsletter—now going out to several thousand people—and within weeks, we had over twenty men in telephone counseling. In addition to all of her other duties, Kathy began counseling hurting wives.

———— ◦•◦ ————

The first two years in Kentucky were extremely difficult

for Kathy and me. We had had our share of problems in Sacramento, but at least there we had the support of family, friends and our church. Now, we were in the middle of rural Kentucky where we didn't know anybody. But hardships continued to break us and to teach us to depend upon the Lord.

Many of these difficulties for me came from unnecessary fretting and illegitimate fears. For instance, I worried about the state shutting the ministry down for code violations. I was also constantly disturbed by the thought of a fire breaking out or someone getting hurt on the property.

The one thing I feared the most was the thought of the people of our neighborhood rising up against us. We had this group of sexual addicts living in the middle of a simple farm community. The somewhat legitimate apprehension that one of our men might victimize someone in the area was bad enough, but to add to the problem were the ridiculous rumors about us that were circulating around the area. Some people said that we were a satanic cult performing human sacrifices. Others were sure that we were operating some kind of prostitution ring. We decided that if we attempted to defend ourselves it would only exacerbate the situation; so we remained silent.

One day, my worst fears were realized. A man running for the office of county administrator decided his campaign theme would be that if he were elected to office, he would "rid the community of this menace," the "menace" being Pure Life Ministries. He took out a huge ad in the local newspaper that asked the question, "Do we have another David Koresh and Waco in our midst?" I discovered that he was going to every single house in our county telling people about us. The truth was enough to cause concern, but he decided to strengthen his case against us by contriving false stories about our men. He said that they had been seen peaking in windows in town, following women home, and so on. I knew he was lying, but I couldn't see any way to convince people who were already leery of us. As if he hadn't done enough damage, he began holding town meetings in an attempt to rouse the anger of the community. To his surprise, I showed up at one of these meetings and confronted him in front of everyone. He was polite but refused to back off his statements. We began to earnestly pray.

Meanwhile, a television station out of Cincinnati heard about the conflict and sent a news team to investigate. The reporter was a Christian who had done a story on the ministry the previous year. He interviewed both parties, and we watched the program with much apprehension. God intervened! The correspondent exposed him for the fraud he was and he lost the election.

Problems in the community were only one kind of attack we had to deal with. There were also spiritual attacks— some of which I wasn't prepared to face. One of these occurred during a trip to Michigan one weekend in 1991. Normally Kathy would travel with me to speaking engagements, but she had developed a backache and decided to stay home. So I had to make the six-hour drive alone. The following week I was scheduled to appear on the *Focus On The Family* radio program.

I made the long drive that day, tempted at times to go into some city and look for pornography, or worse. But I managed to quell those incessant thoughts and made it into Michigan. After filling up my gas tank at a truck stop, I went in to the store to use the restroom. Making my way through the

> *My heart was thumping wildly as I scrambled through the pages. Suddenly, a tiny voice inside me seemed to yell, "Run!"*

store, I noticed a man standing at the magazine rack looking at a "girlie" magazine. I felt a strong attraction to the magazines but really didn't consider actually looking at any. Nevertheless, when I walked by the man, I peered over his shoulder and saw a pornographic layout of some chosen beauty for that month.

That one glimpse of flesh haunted me all weekend. I just couldn't seem to get the image out of my mind. Somehow, I made it through Sunday services, and on Monday morning I started home for Kentucky. As soon as I left the parsonage, my mind drifted back to that truck stop. "No! I will not stop and look at that magazine!" I said out loud. No matter how strong of a stance I tried to take, the picture of the girl continued to plague me. I eventually reached the sign indicating that the off-ramp was one mile away. "I will not stop! I am going on with God!" I shouted. "Glory, hallelujah!"

When the turn-off appeared, I exited the freeway, drove straight to that gas station, went in and saturated my mind with the pictures in that magazine. My heart was thumping wildly as I scrambled through the pages. Suddenly, a tiny voice inside me (the same one I had heard in Los Angeles years before) seemed to yell, "Run!"

Knowing it to be the Holy Spirit, I left immediately and guilt-ridden, I made the long trip back to Kentucky. For the next several days, I continually berated myself. One morning, my self-condemnation reached its peak. "How could you be so stupid? Here you are about to go on national radio, and you have looked at pornography! Stupid!" On and on the self-imposed tirade went.

Before finishing the story, I must refer to an incident that happened to me ten years prior during the last week of the Sheriff's Academy. I had been one of the survivors but still felt as though I had to be careful not to do anything that might disqualify me.

This particular day the cadets were bussed out to the Pomona Fair Grounds to participate in a two-day intensive driving school. There was a high-speed course that was set up with orange parking cones in the vast asphalt area. My turn finally came. The first thing I noticed about the squad car was that it was equipped with a roll cage. A helmet sat on the driving seat awaiting me. "Get in, put on your helmet and take off," said the fearless instructor sitting in the passenger seat.

I did exactly what I was told. I was driving fairly fast when, to my surprise, the instructor yelled out, "faster!" I quickly responded by increasing my speed even more. I was flying around the curves and accelerating on the straightaways. At one particularly difficult curve, I lost control for a second and was forced to drive off of the track. I immediately barreled through the cones again, got back on the roadway and finished out the course. I sat in silence as the instructor filled out his paperwork. Knowing I had gotten off of the track, I moaned, "I guess I failed the course." I was sick inside thinking it might affect my graduating the academy.

"Failed? Why do you think you failed?" he asked.

"I missed that turn and drove right off the track," I lamented.

"Yeah, but you jumped right back on! You did great!" He exclaimed.

So ten years later, as I was on my morning prayer-walk, beating myself for viewing the pornography in the gas station, God spoke to me. In one of those poignant, eternal moments, I relived the incident that occurred a decade before in the squad car. Now it was the Lord speaking. "Steve, you made one little mistake. But you've been doing great! You've been in prayer everyday. You've been pressing in to Me. You've been in the Word faithfully. Yes, you got off

From that day on, I understood that my victory over sin was not because of my efforts but because of God's fabulous grace!

track for a moment, but you jumped right back on!"

I had come into a true revelation of the grace of God. From that day on, I understood that my victory over sin was not because of my efforts but because of God's fabulous grace!

In the meantime, the live-in program continued to grow. That summer the three *Focus On The Family* programs I had appeared on aired, and we got calls from all over the country. One of them was a man named Pete who desperately wanted to come into the live-in program. In his early forties, he had waited many years for a place to go to overcome sexual sin. His determination to find victory was obvious. He left New Mexico in his Chevy pick-up and hadn't gotten a hundred miles when his transmission began acting up. He drove nearly 1,500 miles in second gear!

Many men came and went through the live-in program. During those early days, about half that entered the program either quit or were asked to leave before completion. Later, as things got better, it became fairly rare that anyone would leave prematurely.

Within no time, the live-in program grew to 17 men—all living in that little farmhouse! Something had to be done. We began praying for the Lord to give us a better

> *I went forward, and as soon as my knees hit the floor at the altar, I began to weep. All I could see was my pride and self-centeredness.*

piece of property. We also concluded that it would be good to become involved in a local church.

One Sunday in November 1991, Kathy, Lance and I visited an Assembly of God church located in a small town nearby. We decided to check it out in the hopes that it would be a good church for our men to attend.

The Lord used the pastor's sermon from Luke 6 to show me that I was not living in the love of Christ toward others. I was not stirred emotionally, but I felt convicted. As he concluded his sermon, he invited those who felt that they needed to get right with God to come forward. In my prideful condition, the last thing I wanted to do was to respond to an altar call. I was there to check the church out, not to repent! In spite of my reluctance, I knew that I had to obey the Lord's voice.

I went forward, and as soon as my knees hit the floor at the altar, I began to weep. All I could see was my pride and self-centeredness. I saw the lack of mercy and love in my life. The more God showed me, the more I wept. Pretty soon deep sobs were wracking my whole frame. In front of this entire congregation, which I had been so concerned about impressing, I was blubbering like a baby! The more I cried, the more humiliated I felt. The more humiliated I felt, the more I cried.

It was a terrible experience in the flesh and yet was one of the greatest days in my life! My prideful thinking, selfish nature, and stubborn will were all dealt a severe, but precise, blow. Out of that experience came a new brokenness that greatly affected the way I treated the men.

———————

Not long after this, our real estate agent telephoned to ask me if we would be interested in a farm on 45 acres that was for sale. We were in a tough situation. We had 17 men living in our house (complete with a urinal in the closet!), and it would have been very difficult to show it to perspective buyers. Yes, I was definitely interested in looking at another property—one that would be big enough for future expansion—but how would we ever sell the place on 12 acres?

In spite of my reservations, we went to look at the farm. It had been called Fairview because it sat on top of a high ridge and had been built prior to the outbreak of the Civil War. We fell in love with it as soon as we saw it. The big, white pillars in the front gave it the look of an old plantation. We really wanted it, but I couldn't imagine how we could possibly purchase it. We didn't have any money for a down payment and could not qualify for a bank loan. On top of all of that, we still had the other property to deal with. It seemed impossible, but we began intently praying.

The real estate broker offered a possible solution. He would buy back the house we had purchased from him and give us back—not the $10,000 we had given him as a down payment—but the $17,000 the seller of Fairview wanted as a down payment. Because there were better terms on the loan with the Fairview property, our payment would only be $80 more per month! It was a marvelous answer to prayer. Again, God made a way for us where there seemed to be no way.

By this time, Pete (who had made the cross-country trip in second gear) had graduated the program and come to work for us as a maintenance man. Much work needed to be done before we could move the men into the new property. We had the mobile home moved over to the new site and again did most of the work to set it up ourselves. We then had to install a new septic tank and cistern and had to build a bathroom for over twenty men. Next, we—Pete, myself and another guy—constructed a two-story addition to the house that provided more bedrooms upstairs and a large dining room downstairs. No sooner had we moved to the new location than we received a flurry of new applications. Soon we had 26 men in the live-in program!

One day, I received a phone call from an old friend. He told me about a Major League baseball player named Jack whose successful career had fallen apart because of his addiction to sex and crack cocaine. The crack had caused him to become so paranoid that he was living in a friend's closet with a loaded gun. He wanted to know if we could help him.

When I called Jack the next day, he seemed like a little kid, scared and broken. My heart went out to him as we talked. I tried to sound tough with him to let him know that he would not be given special privileges at Pure Life. Jack was so full of fear though, that I found myself encouraging him. "Why don't you get on a plane, Jack," I urged him. "If you really want the Lord, you will find Him here in a very special way."

Kathy was not so optimistic about the whole thing. "I was very concerned that some of the men in the program would be star-struck and lose track of why they were there, but Steve was unwilling to turn him away," she recalls. "His argument was that Jack was as valuable to God as the other men, and he deserved a chance, too."

He arrived about a week later. He looked terrible. It

was easy to see he had lost a lot of weight from his playing days. Totally at the end of himself and almost insane by this time, Jack responded immediately to

Even though his entire life had fallen apart, he remained essentially unbroken.

the message of God's mercy which is stressed at Pure Life. It began to touch his life in a wonderful way. The Lord's presence was changing him and healing his mind. This started the process of restoring what the drugs and the sex had destroyed. His time spent in the Word of God every day literally brought sanity to his fearful, tormented mind.

But it soon became clear to us that Jack's greatest problem was not greed, nor worldliness, nor even his obsession with sex. His great, besetting sin was the inordinate amount of pride that had been fostered and nurtured by years of stardom. Even though his entire life had fallen apart, he remained essentially unbroken. As he regained his "sanity," his pride began to rear its ugly head at Pure Life.

At first, it was just over trivial things. He did not like the rules in the live-in program and would simply disregard those which he thought were unnecessary. There is a 10 p.m. curfew in the facility, but if he wanted to eat a snack or talk to one of the other guys, he would do it. When approached about his noncompliant behavior, he would minimize it or shrug it off. As time went on, he grew more arrogant and rebellious. After several months of working with him, Lance finally attempted a desperate move: he had what is coined a "light session" with him during the Tuesday evening accountability meeting. With Jack sitting there center stage, each man in the program was asked to share his perspective on the ballplayer's walk with God. Every single man said that he was extremely prideful.

Jack did not like this very much, but he remained silent. The staff continued to fervently pray for him, hoping that this incident would help turn him around. Unfortunately, his behavior continued to deteriorate after this. Although he was two weeks away from completing the program, I knew I could not graduate a man who was so hard-hearted and unbroken. I reluctantly called him into my office and told him he would have to leave the facility.

Of course, my hope was that he would be immediately shocked into repentance. This was a last ditch effort to reach him. Indeed, over the years I have seen a number of men come to this fork in the road and burst into tears, pleading with me to allow them to stay. Unfortunately, Jack didn't repent; he got angry. It was obvious that he was not accustomed to people crossing his will like that. He exploded in a rage. "Oh, you're just like the rest, Steve!" he roared. "I hear a lot about mercy around here—but I don't see any!" He then stormed out and slammed the door so hard that it split the wood on the frame. I sat there in tears. I had had so much hope for Jack, but in the end, he did what all rebels do: he turned against the one who was attempting to help him. Eight months later he died of a drug overdose.

Eleven

THE FAITH HOMES

The tremendous breaking I received at the altar of that small Pentecostal church did much to soften my attitude toward others. However, I still often lapsed into the miserable mindset that had plagued me my entire life and many times was difficult to work with. Sometimes I would even lash out in anger at those around me. My problems actually went deeper than that, though. It wasn't simply my difficult nature. Something was clearly missing in my life.

I wasn't the only one who felt this lack. Kathy and Lance were aware of it in their lives as well. "Where is the bubbling fountain of life? Where is the abundant life promised to all believers in Christ? Where is the all-consuming love for God and others? Where is the joy of the Lord?" We couldn't understand why our spiritual lives seemed so dry and lifeless.

Over a period of months, we continually cried out to God for Him to do something for us. We remained faithful to our daily devotions and trusted the Lord to answer our pleas for help.

During the spring of 1992, I flew to California to preach at a large Assembly of God church in San Jose. A group of men from a local Teen Challenge center (a ministry to drug addicts that had acquired fame through the book *The Cross and the Switchblade*) were in the congregation that night. James Thomas, the pastor of their facility, invited me to come and minister to their men. He and his wife had once been junkies in New York City. They got saved in the early 1960s and came up through the ranks of the original Teen Challenge Center with David Wilkerson.

I enjoyed my time with them, and as I prepared to leave, he excitedly told me about a ministry located in the Midwest called the Faith Homes. He gave me a book they used entitled, *What The Bible Teaches About Mercy* written by the late Rex Andrews, who had been a minister there. I knew I needed more mercy in my life, so I agreed to read it. He also told me about a couple named Doug and Millie, whom he had worked with at the Brooklyn Teen Challenge Center.

Although there were nine ministers on staff at the Faith Homes, Doug and Millie were recognized as the leaders. Doug had graduated from Harvard with honors, and Millie had graduated from a Nazarene college in Massachusetts. In 1965, right after they were married, they moved to New York City and went to work at Teen Challenge. Millie became secretary first to Leonard Ravenhill, and then to David Wilkerson, while Doug worked with the men. Nearly two years later, they felt as though it was time for them to move on, so they began exploring different options. Having been a part of the exciting work God was doing in New York made them attractive as potential employees, and before they knew it, they had invitations for employment from nine different ministries and organizations.

As they prayed over these different opportunities, someone made them aware of the Faith Homes. They were told it was a ministry that emphasized prayer, and that surely they would be humbled if they went there to live. The Lord led them to turn down every other offer and to enter the Faith Homes. They were thinking, "We're pretty worn out from our

As they began their internship there, they quickly realized that their knowledge of God was very limited and superficial.

work at Teen Challenge; perhaps after a six month rest, we'll look again for a place to minister." In time, everything pointed to this small, obscure ministry as the place God wanted them to be, not for rest, but for more training, and eventually to join the staff.

What Doug and Millie did not understand in those early days was the depth of spirituality and knowledge of God that was in the Faith Homes. Yes, with their credentials and experience they could have landed a job in ministry almost anywhere. However, at the Faith Homes, those things mattered very little. The primary focus was upon the need for a person to be conquered inside by the Holy Spirit. As they began their internship there, they quickly realized that their knowledge of God was very limited and superficial. This painful reality was brought home by the very fact that they were trainees there for 6½ years before they were ordained as ministers. This was certainly not a flashy or shallow ministry! For this reason, I was interested in finding out more about it.

When I arrived home in Kentucky, I began reading through the book about mercy. I also asked different people I knew if they had heard of this ministry. Several ministers told me that the Lord made Himself very real to people at the Faith Homes. One friend told me, "The reason His voice can be heard more clearly there is primarily because of the deep level of consecration the ministers live in who run the place. If you want to learn about real Christianity, that's the

> *Despite my recent experience of brokenness, my selfishness and pride stood out in stark contrast to the way they demonstrated the love of Christ to other people.*

place to go!" I asked a missionary friend if he had ever heard of the place, and he told me in a hushed tone that it was a "powerhouse" where one could sense the Spirit of God in a dramatic way. Another pastor said that as soon as he walked through the front door he felt the Holy Spirit searching his heart, exposing sin, selfishness, pride, or questionable motives of his heart.

It sounded like the very thing we needed. Kathy, Lance and I didn't know what to expect the first time we visited the Faith Homes. Would the people be super-spiritual weirdos, out of touch with the realities of life? Or would they be in such close contact with God that they could read our thoughts? When we arrived there that summer day in 1992, these and other questions filled our minds.

The Faith Homes consisted of three, beautifully maintained Victorian homes located in a quiet community in Zion, Illinois. About a block from each other, each house had its own trainees and served its own particular function. We stayed at the guest home where Doug and Millie lived.

We were greatly relieved to find the people there—ministers, workers and trainees—to be the nicest, most ordinary folks we could have imagined. We did not get the sense that they were strange or cultish at all. In fact, as the days rolled by, we began to see their humility and unselfishness in a thousand different little ways. Despite my recent experience of brokenness, my selfishness and pride stood out in stark contrast to the way they demonstrated the love of Christ to other people.

We became convinced that the kind of relationship they had with the Lord was what we had been longing for. There was an abundance of life in their Christian experience that we had never seen before. I realized that we were witnessing the sort of Christianity Paul described throughout his writings. I was fed up with dry, powerless religion and was determined to have what they possessed.

During our stay there we were able to enjoy lengthy and meaningful discussions about our Christian life with Doug during mealtimes. We were especially interested to hear his perspective about what it was that we were missing. Over and over again he reiterated that the abundant life comes from living out the love of God toward other people. This was primarily done through meeting their needs. The more he talked about love, grace and mercy, the more it became clear to me that over the years in ministry I had built walls up with people who used such terms. Too often I had seen sloppy, humanistic mercy being portrayed as godly love and licentiousness being promoted under the term grace. Yet, when Doug spoke about such subjects, there was a reality in his words. These people were living in a level of consecration to God that we didn't have and yet, at the same time, they were full of love and joy.

Those "table talks" were just as fascinating as the meetings because it was there that we could become involved in deep and fascinating conversations about the kingdom of God. Unfortunately, I was still very much full of myself. In spite of my serious nature, I had a certain California flippancy that seemed to gush out at the most inopportune times. On the one hand, I was hungry to hear these ministers reveal some of the mysteries of God. However, just as often I would make wisecracks and draw attention to myself.

One day, Doug asked if he could talk to me. We went

into a side room and he gently told me that he needed to speak to me about my table manners. "Steve, we want this place to be full of the atmosphere of God. In a very real way we consider the Holy Spirit to be a guest in this place. That's why you love it here. But when you enter the room, suddenly the room is filled with the personality of Steve Gallagher." His reproof was given very humbly, but it went into me like a knife. I knew what he was saying was true and felt terrible that I would do anything to disrupt that heavenly atmosphere. After that I exercised more control over my tongue.

Our five days ended much too quickly, and we made the seven-hour drive back to Kentucky on Sunday. Nevertheless, we left there flooded with hope that we had stumbled upon a spiritual goldmine.

The reason we had to get home was because CBS was sending a reporter, producer and film crew to the ministry to film a piece on Pure Life for their *48 Hours* program. They were going to devote a show to the pornography issue in America and wanted to air a segment about those who had been addicted to it.

As we spent Monday preparing for the film crew to arrive the following morning, I pondered the things we had been told at the Homes. It all sounded so promising, but I still didn't know how living a life of mercy would affect my life.

Tuesday morning, I went out on my customary prayer walk. We were scheduled to have our weekly staff prayer meeting at 8:00. The television crew was due to arrive at 9:00. While I was walking around praising the Lord in the hayfield out

> *In one second, the concept flooded my mind: the entire realm of God's kingdom revolves around His mercy!*

back, I suddenly received a tremendous revelation from God. It was as if there had been a logjam in my mind about what I had been taught regarding mercy. In one second, the concept flooded my mind: *the entire realm of God's kingdom revolves around His mercy!* It was no longer simply a teaching or a notion; it was a living reality inside me.

God is love and that love is manifested to mankind through mercy—meeting the needs of others. When a believer begins to help other people, he places himself in the flow of God's love. He becomes a channel for the power and grace of God to be extended to others. I thought about all the biographies of Christian ministers I had read. William Carey was God's mercy to the dark continent of India. George Mueller was raised up to care for the orphans of England. David Wilkerson was used by the Lord to help the drug addicts and gang members of New York City. Every story I could think of had this same element: God was living out His love through some saint by meeting the needs of those he had been sent to help.

As I made my way back from the hayfield, it occurred to me that we had our "field of mercy" right there on our property. Men bound up in sexual sin were to be the recipients of God's love through the staff. We were meeting their needs as we helped them overcome their life-controlling habits. When I realized all of this, it was as if I comprehended Christianity for the first time in my life.

In the meantime, the staff had become a little concerned about me. It was 8:15, and I still hadn't shown up for our meeting. This was very uncharacteristic for someone who is usually very punctual. When I did arrive, I had the brightest smile that Kathy had ever seen on my face. All I could say, over and over again, was, "It's all mercy! It's all mercy!" I could not contain my joy. The lights had come on inside

> *The Lord can do far more through the life of one man who is genuinely on fire for God than through the lives of thousands who are content with mediocrity.*

me, revealing the prison of SELF I had lived in my entire life. The secret was to get out of myself and to truly become involved in the lives of others.

Before long the film crew arrived. They interviewed Kathy, myself and several of the men. They took some film clips of the property and the men eating supper, and then they left.

Looking at that day from an outward perspective, it seemed that being filmed for a popular television show viewed by millions of viewers was a huge milestone for Pure Life Ministries. Indeed, when it aired a couple of months later, we were inundated with telephone calls from people wanting to come into the live-in program. No doubt the Lord used that program in ways we will never know about until we reach heaven.

However, the effects on the ministry from the airing of that program were only felt over a period of a few months. By contrast, what occurred inside me out in the hayfield altered the entire course of my life and ministry. The revelation I received about the love of God that morning has steadily grown within me ever since. Furthermore, not only has it changed my life, it has in turn affected the lives of the Pure Life staff and also the hundreds of men we have ministered to down through the years since then.

It also taught me a huge lesson: in the Kingdom of God, depth is more important than size. The Lord can do far more through the life of one man who is genuinely on fire for God than through the lives of thousands who are content with mediocrity. I should have learned that as I read about the lives of men like Hudson Taylor and William Carey. So often today, Christians are impressed with the size of an organization, how many radio stations that air a minister's sermons, or the number of people in a pastor's congregation. It isn't that having a large ministry is a bad thing. However, I began to understand that, just because an organization is big and seems to be doing more, does not necessarily mean that it is accomplishing anything worthwhile spiritually. In the Kingdom of God quality counts far more than quantity.

Likewise, I came to see that the heart-felt cries rising to God from a handful of consecrated, godly people who were living sacrificially for others could have more of a spiritual impact on our country than the work of a huge organization manned by compromising believers fixated on worldly techniques and ideas.

1993 was a year of building for the ministry. We were able, with the help of a contractor who was a student in the live-in program, to construct a new office building. Our headquarters had been upstairs in the tiny rooms of the addition to the main house. Now we were finally able to move the shipping department and business telephone lines into a bona-fide office setting.

There was one more building project we needed to undertake. Kathy and I had been living in an 8 by 32-foot camping trailer on the property for 18 months. As difficult as it was for her, Kathy never complained. She simply did her best to make it a home. We constructed a modest, two-bedroom house on the ministry grounds for us to live in. For the four-plus years since we had left Sacramento, we had lived in a motor home, a one-bedroom trailer, a small apartment and then the camping trailer. We were so excited that one would have thought we were moving into a 5,000 square-foot mansion!

All of this was beneficial, but the real building going on in the ministry was spiritual. God was doing a deep work in all of us that started from the top down. The Spirit of Mercy was getting into us and was completely changing our lives. Not only were we all becoming kinder and more loving, we were beginning to live in the joy we had seen in the ministers of the Faith Home.

Over the coming months, Kathy and I began making two, three, and even four-week trips to the Homes. When we visited, we took the role of trainees scrubbing dishes, floors, and toilets, and waiting on other guests. For the first time in our Christian lives, we learned what it meant to serve others. Although we ran a ministry that was arguably more prominent than the Faith Homes, we knew we needed to be taught how to love others. If that meant that we had to be trainees, so be it.

This did not come easily for me, however. I had a lot of pride and did not like being treated like a servant. This high-minded attitude became very real to me during one particular Sunday afternoon meal at the Faith Homes. I had grown accustomed to sitting next to Doug at the head of the table, where he and I would have profound discussions. However, visitors were often invited to eat dinner at the Homes after church. Doug, always the gracious host, seated the guests near him so that he could give them his undivided attention. This left me relegated to the other end of the table. On top of that, I had to serve dinner and clean up the dishes.

I felt very insignificant that day. I didn't want to be a server! I wanted to be served. My attitude was unlike Jesus in so many ways. He said, "Whoever wishes to become great among you shall be your servant, and whoever wishes to be first among you shall be your slave; just as the Son of Man did not come to be served, but to serve, and to give His life a

The Lord was helping me to see that the Kingdom of God is not like the world. The highest position in His realm is that of servant.

ransom for many." (Matthew 20:26-28) My pride stood out glaringly. Even though my flesh cringed during the entire meal, I performed my duties. As I was seated at the end of the table, a verse came into my mind very forcefully. "But let the brother of humble circumstances glory in his high position." (James 1:9) The Lord was helping me to see that the Kingdom of God is not like the world. The highest position in His realm is that of servant.

These kinds of experiences were completely overthrowing the self-centered perspective of ministry I had held over the years. While the Lord was constantly humbling us, He was also giving us a sight into His Kingdom that was breathtaking at times. It was as if we would go to the Homes to get a sight of the Lord and then would have to go back to Pure Life to get that knowledge worked into us through the trials and tribulations of ministry. Nevertheless, every time we left there, we felt as though we loved God more than before. David's words came to life there for us: "For a day in Thy courts is better than a thousand outside. I would rather stand at the threshold of the house of my God, than dwell in the tents of wickedness." (Psalm 84:10)

One never knew what would occur at the Faith Homes. God's presence was so strong at times that anything could happen. During one service, Kathy was quietly flipping through the pages of the hymnal and came upon the old song, "Spirit of God Descend Upon My Heart." The words are very precious and were obviously written by a person who knew the Lord intimately. Those lyrics perfectly described the cry inside Kathy's heart for a greater infilling of the Holy Spirit. She meditated upon each stanza, relishing the profound insights of the dear saint who had written it. Of course, the strong sense of God's nearness breathed life into those words. As she was quietly praying, the congregation began singing that very song! It was the Lord's way of letting Kathy know that He was hearing the cry of her heart.

Another manifestation of how the Lord was there in a very real way was in reading the Word of God. I had always loved the Scriptures and had learned while in Bible school to turn to them for the solutions to life's problems. However, the Bible was often more like a textbook I turned to in search of answers than an experience of God's heart and character. This all changed while I was at the Faith Homes. There, the Scriptures came alive to me. There were times I would be sitting in my room reading, and the words seemed to jump off the page into my heart. There was such a reality to what was being expressed. Jesus said, "It is the Spirit who gives life; the flesh profits nothing; the words that I have spoken to you are spirit and are life." (John 6:63) For the first time I understood what He meant.

Corrie Ten Boom had this same experience in Ravensbruck Concentration Camp. There in that dismal world filled with hatred and suffering, Scripture came to life. She said, "Sometimes I would slip the Bible from its little sack with hands that shook, so mysterious had it become to me. It was new; it had just been written. I marveled sometimes that the ink was dry."[1]

One such incident occurred during a Monday evening meeting. As usual, everybody in the congregation sat in silence for a time before the meeting began. "What a wonderful way to begin a meeting," I thought to myself. "Having the people spend that time quietly waiting on God instead of socializing with others."

However, this meeting would prove to be different

In the meantime, Kathy was having her own encounter with the Almighty. To this day she does not know exactly what happened to her.

than any other we had attended. Kathy and I arrived twenty minutes early and silently prayed. When the meeting should have begun, none of the ministers moved. Kathy and I continued to seek the Lord privately.

As the minutes rolled by, the presence of God seemed to intensify. For quite some time I simply sat there enjoying Him. After awhile I decided to read my Bible. I opened it randomly to First Corinthians. The following words jumped off the page with such force that I knew God was speaking to me: "For who regards you as superior? And what do you have that you did not receive? But if you did receive it, why do you boast as if you had not received it?" The words went through my heart as the Lord confronted me about spiritual pride. I read on: "Now some have become arrogant, as though I were not coming to you. But I will come to you soon, if the Lord wills, and I shall find out, not the words of those who are arrogant, but their power. For the kingdom of God does not consist in words, but in power. What do you desire? Shall I come to you with a rod or with love and a spirit of gentleness?" (I Corinthians 4:7, 18-21) I felt thoroughly chastised by the Lord and yet, I also sensed His love behind the discipline.

In the meantime, Kathy was having her own encounter with the Almighty. To this day she does not know exactly what happened to her. "I just felt like God was doing a deep work inside me that night," she recalls. Indeed, she wept through most of that service.

After nearly two hours of silence, one of the ministers finally went to the podium and closed the meeting in prayer. I don't know what happened for others that evening, but Kathy and I were both deeply affected.

The effects of these experiences continued to build something inside us that has remained for years. It was as if God deposited a fresh revelation about Himself within us during every visit. We became absolutely enthralled with Him. At the end of each stay, we would leave with much reluctance. There was a ministry to run and men who needed help. Little did we know then what still lay ahead.

---

[1] Corrie Ten Boom, *The Hiding Place*, Chosen Books, NY, 1971, p. 178

Twelve

DEEPER REVELATIONS

*D*r. Avi Greenburg—a Jewish believer from New York—was one of the men in the live-in program that needed our attention. He had discovered his father's collection of pornographic magazines when he was ten years old. The effects of seeing those images remained with him for years to come. He describes his struggle to find answers to life's problems:

> In 1980, I received my Ph.D. The status of holding a doctorate fed my pride, but to my disappointment, I did not find the answers I was seeking in psychology. I embraced secular humanism, believing that man had within himself basic goodness and the key to self-fulfillment; yet most of my colleagues seemed as broken in their personal lives as I felt in mine. Something wasn't right.

Upon receiving his doctorate, Avi's first job was as a counselor in an addictions treatment center. He rarely used drugs anymore, but his obsession with pornography continued. He

> *"Through the live-in program at Pure Life, I recognized that the real core of my problem was not psychological; it was in my sin nature."*

married not long after graduating. Unfortunately, his pornography addiction caused him to remain emotionally detached from his new wife.

After a couple of years of marriage, he finally confessed to his wife that he regularly viewed pornography. He knew he needed to do something about it. He found out about Pure Life Ministries and entered the live-in program. What he received during his six-month stay was far different than what he was accustomed to:

> The first thing I had to come to grips with was the fact that eight years of schooling didn't provide me with the answers I needed for true fulfillment or even victory over my own compulsive behavior. As a Christian, I knew my behavior was sinful, but as a psychologist, I always believed that if I could just get to the core of the psychological conflicts in my past, I would develop the insight necessary to resolve the emotional conflicts I experienced. I was sure this insight combined with the background I had in 12-step programs and techniques would be enough to change my behavior. The change I needed, though, was a heart change.
>
> Through the live-in program at Pure Life, I recognized that the real core of my problem was not psychological; it was in my sin nature. The real solution, then, could only come through true repentance and developing a practical daily lifestyle of discipleship and accountability. By learning to die to the flesh

and live by the Spirit, I finally experienced victory over sexual sin.

———•———

Through the influence of the Faith Homes, we were learning how to better help men like Avi. We learned three elements of ministry there that revolutionized our counseling. The first was the immense importance of dealing with the men in the proper balance of love and truth. If we over-emphasized truth, the man would become beaten down and discouraged by the overwhelming reality of his sinful condition. By the same token, if we were overly sympathetic and encouraging, he would inevitably gravitate back into his old carnal mindset. What this man desperately needed was someone who would truly love him and yet also stand against his flesh. Once a man came to see that we sincerely cared about him, he could handle the occasional reproof that would come his way when he started drifting off course. The correction was the part of the counseling process that helped him stay on track. The love he received from us was what made the reproof tolerable. If we overemphasized either love or truth the outcome could be disastrous. However, when we kept the two in balance, the results were often astounding.

The second thing that we learned—especially through their teachings on the subject of mercy—was the importance of real discipleship.* It was imperative that these struggling men have someone in their lives who would bear them spiritually. When Paul spoke of helping those who were struggling with sin, he said, "Bear one another's burdens,

---

* I've become convinced that one of the primary reasons there is so much worldliness and spiritual immaturity in the Church is that pastors have become more focused on "church growth" rather than "Christian growth."

> *They were coming to us for help—some of them with everything on the line—and we did not dare treat that responsibility lightly.*

and thus fulfill the law of Christ." (Galatians 6:2) This meant that we had to become involved in their lives in a very real way. We had to take their problems and struggles upon ourselves. We had to be there for them when they needed us, and most importantly, we had to bear them to God in prayer—much prayer.* How would they ever find freedom if there was no one to intercede for them?

The other truth that became very real to us at the Homes was our duty to have something of spiritual value to offer these men. They were coming to us for help—some of them with everything on the line—and we did not dare treat that responsibility lightly. One of the things I was taught there was that I could only bring another as far as I had gone myself. If I only had a superficial walk with the Lord, that was all I could ever hope to give others. I realized that pressing into God was not simply so I could enjoy His presence for myself—as important as that may be. I owed it to these men to grow spiritually so that I might better help them.

This determination to increase the level of spiritual maturity at PLM was part of the reason we began sending our staff members for two-week visits to the Homes every three months. Kathy and I continued to go there for lengthy stays as well. God continued to unfold new truths about Himself to us each time we went there. He also dealt with us relentlessly about our selfishness and pride.

One thing the Lord started confronting me about was

---

* There are plenty of teachers abounding today who write books and teach seminars about overcoming sexual addiction. How few there are who are willing to bear those who struggle.

the fact that Pure Life Ministries had become an idol in my heart. Rather than attempting to draw near to the Lord during my prayer times, I spent my time trying to convince Him that He needed to advance PLM. This wrong attitude led to constant fretting. Instead of trusting the Lord to provide for our finances, our workers, and our future, I took all of this upon myself.

Deep inside I was still driven by a self-centered ambition for the ministry. Pure Life was merely an extension of Steve Gallagher. If the ministry became successful, then I could feel that my life had meaning and significance. If it failed, it meant that I was a failure. I constantly worried about things that could destroy the organization.

It didn't take long for Doug to discern the heavy pressure I was putting upon myself. On one of my visits there, he gave me an old A. B. Simpson song to read. "Steve, I want you to spend at least an hour meditating on this song," he told me. "It will do a lot to help you. Ask the Lord to make the words real to you."

Himself

Once it was the blessing, Now it is the Lord;
Once it was the feeling, Now it is His Word;
Once His gift I wanted, Now, the Giver own;
Once I sought for healing, Now Himself alone.

Once 'twas painful trying, Now 'tis perfect trust;
Once a half salvation, Now the uttermost;
Once 'twas ceaseless holding, Now He holds me fast;
Once 'twas constant drifting, Now my anchor's cast.

Once 'twas busy planning, Now 'tis trustful prayer;
Once 'twas anxious caring, Now He has the care;

Once 'twas what I wanted, Now what Jesus says;
Once 'twas constant asking, Now 'tis ceaseless praise.

Once it was my working, His it hence shall be;
Once I tried to use Him, Now He uses me;
Once the pow'r I wanted, Now the Mighty One;
Once for self I labored, Now for Him alone.

Once I hoped in Jesus, Now I know He's mine;
Once my lamps were dying, Now they brightly shine;
Once for death I waited, Now His coming hail;
And my hopes are anchored safe within the vail.

Chorus
All in all forever, Jesus will I sing;
Everything in Jesus, and Jesus every thing.

I went to my room and prayed over each stanza. The Lord used these words of testimony to show me that my relationship to Him was very skewed. Rather than truly loving Him and others, I was using Him to achieve status. This began a work in my heart that would continue for a long time.

On another visit to the Homes, several of the ministers had to leave town and Doug asked me to speak in the Sunday evening service. I was both frightened and excited at the same time. It would be such an honor to speak there, but what could I possibly have to share with people who seemed to be light years ahead of me in the Christian journey?

That Sunday evening service was opened with some very worshipful songs. I was then invited to come to the podium. When I would speak in churches, there was an intensity to my preaching that would seem to have a heavy anointing from the Lord. I had sub-consciously learned to rely upon this to make my messages seem "powerful." So as I began speaking at the Faith Homes that evening, I followed my normal course of becoming in-

The harder I preached, the more pronounced the barrier seemed to become. It was as if God Himself was standing right in front of me.

creasingly strong and loud. I would soon discover that this was not the typical church.

As I was preaching, I could feel a mysterious invisible wall form one inch from my face. The harder I preached, the more pronounced the barrier seemed to become. It was as if God Himself was standing right in front of me. Every word I spoke seemed to hit that wall and fall straight to the floor. Everything I said sounded so empty and futile. I felt like there was no substance to what I was telling them. Perhaps the best explanation of it would be found in the words of Jude who wrote of teachers who were "clouds without wa-ter..." Or maybe a better description is found in the book of Proverbs: "Like the legs which hang down from the lame, so is a proverb in the mouth of fools." (Proverbs 26:9)

I felt a growing conviction that it would be much better for everybody if I would just sit down. I couldn't finish my talk quickly enough and practically ran to my seat when I finished. It didn't help matters when Kathy leaned over to me and whispered, "I didn't think you would ever sit down!"

"Was it that bad?" I asked. She confirmed that it was. She had also been humiliated. Although we were stunned by the incident, the people in the meeting seemed to be com-pletely unaware of any of this. A number of them expressed their gratitude for what I had shared. I didn't know if they were just being gracious or if they were simply oblivious to

> *Somehow I understood that I was being shown how insignificant I am in the grand scheme of life.*

what I had gone through. I cringed with every compliment and left as quickly as I could.

When we got back to the guesthouse, I shared my humiliation with one of the trainees and asked for his feedback on what I shared in the meeting. To my surprise, he was *also* blessed by the message. When I shared with him my perspective of what happened, he exclaimed knowingly, "Oh! You tried to storm the mic'!"

"What does that mean?" I asked.

"That's when you try to steal God's glory. Didn't you know you couldn't do that here?"

"I guess I needed to learn the hard way," I lamely replied.

Even though it was very humbling, it was also a wonderful experience for me. God was teaching me how to minister with the right motive and in the right spirit—His Spirit.

Another painful incident occurred to me after I had attended a Monday night service at the Faith Homes. In an unexplainable way, God was making me feel very weak and "needy" inside. The old feelings of rejection seemed to wash over me like black waves. I returned to the guesthouse and went directly to bed. All night long I tossed and turned in a fitful, half-sleep. Sometime in the midst of this I had a dream—perhaps vision is a more accurate term—where I was led to the edge of a bottomless pit. The Lord compelled me to look into it. Somehow I understood that I was being shown how insignificant I am in the grand scheme of life. That bottomless pit represented the emptiness of what I had to offer others outside of God.

I eventually fell asleep and the next morning asked Doug if I could speak with him. I was confused about what had happened and was looking for his advice. However, there was something much deeper going on inside me. I was very upset but did not know why. We went into a room to talk, and I couldn't even get words out of my mouth. I simply crumpled to the floor in a heap of tears. Doug later made the statement that it was the clearest example of a person who was utterly undone over himself that he had ever witnessed in all his years of ministry. God was correcting, purifying and breaking me every time I turned around. But, through it all, He made His love very real to me.

Kathy was having her own encounters with God as well. Doug was preaching one Sunday morning about how Jesus was so willing to identify Himself with sinners. He was talking about the time when Jesus stood in line with the publicans, prostitutes and drunkards waiting to be baptized by John. The Pharisees scowled at all of them from a distance. As Doug was talking about the lowliness of the Lord, suddenly—only for a split second—Kathy found herself there along the Jordan River witnessing the whole event. As quickly as the vision appeared it vanished.

It was a week later before she even told me about it. What she experienced was more of an all-encompassing sensation than something simply seen. Part of it was an overwhelming sense of peace. "Until that happened, I had no idea how much fear and insecurity people are engulfed in," she recalls. "For one instant, I got a glimpse of the utter absence of fear there will be in heaven. I simply do not have the words to describe what that was like." Perhaps that is what the apostle Paul meant when he said that he "was caught up into Paradise, and heard inexpressible words..." (II Corinthians 12:4)

Over the months, the Lord continued to reveal Himself to her through that vision. As He would draw near to her, she would feel the same wonderful sensation of His presence she felt that day. One time, as we were standing in a parking lot in Alaska, she became enveloped in the reality that heaven doesn't contain God but *is* God. Everything about that vision always led Kathy to humble herself before the Lord.

Kathy only shared this incident with a couple of very close friends. I was not so wise. Not long after it happened, I made the mistake of telling some of the guys in the program about it. It quickly became obvious that they did not have the spiritual maturity to handle such a story. They asked questions like, "What color was Jesus' hair?" They completely missed the profound import of what had occurred.

Some believers who have never had such encounters with God cringe when they hear others speak of them. I myself become suspicious when people tell of having visions and experiences if I get the sense that they are attempting to bring attention or glory to themselves. On the other hand, I never want to be like the Pharisees who were so rigid and closed-minded that they couldn't receive the new thing that God was doing.

Deeper life experiences are never meant to take the place of the Word of God or the disciplines of the daily Christian life. However, they certainly can help a person to fall more deeply in love with Christ. Over a century ago, one of *The Pulpit Commentary* writers made this statement: "Those seasons in which God approaches most near to the soul, and communicates most directly with us, are momentous; they constitute epochs in our spiritual history."[1] As Kathy and I have surveyed our Christian

> *I needed my heart to be infused with God's great love because I just didn't have it in myself.*

journey, we see that different events in our lives—whether it was a mountain-top ecstasy or deep sorrow and brokenness—have played a major part in shaping us into who we are today.

———•———

As time went on, I continued to become more deeply affected by my experiences at the Faith Homes. It wasn't merely the visits there that were influencing me but also Andrews' book, *What the Bible Teaches About Mercy*,[2] and the taped messages they offered that taught through it. I listened to those tapes over and over. I needed my heart to be infused with God's great love because I just didn't have it in myself. Over time, the reality and significance of His love for people took root within me.

The other book that Rex Andrews had written was entitled, *Meditations in the Revelation*,[3] which I started studying in early 1993. It was just as profound as his study on the subject of mercy. "The book of Revelation was written by someone who was deeply, deeply in love with Jesus. It cannot be properly understood through an academic mindset," Doug said one time. Reading Andrews' study created a hunger in me to study this apocalyptic book of the Bible.

I became gripped by this study. I had routinely studied books of the Bible at length, but none of these studies could be compared to this one. All total, I spent over twelve hundred hours scrutinizing every verse and chapter of Revelation. I listened to sermons on tape, read books, pored over commentaries, studied it inductively, prayed over the verses, one by one, and listened to a dramatization of the book on cassette so many times the tape was worn out.

Most of the contemporary books seemed fairly shallow to me compared to the riches I found in older works such as

The Pulpit Commentary. God put a hunger for truth in my heart that drove me on. Studying this tremendous book literally became a full-time job; I would usually spend forty hours a week in this study.

As month after month rolled by during that time, a picture of what the Lord is presenting in the Revelation started forming in my mind. An archeologist who discovers an ancient plaque could illustrate the process I underwent. As he carefully goes about the tedious job of brushing away the dirt and grime that has become caked on the relic over the centuries, an image gradually begins to emerge.

For me too, as I spent time in this tremendous book of mysteries, a message began to emerge which affected me very deeply. I became increasingly aware of how the spirit of this world is affecting the minds and hearts of Christians.* All these years later, my life has been eternally changed by that Bible study. There was a great call from God imparted to my soul that still affects me to this day: "Come out of her, my people, that you may not participate in her sins and that you may not receive of her plagues; for her sins have piled up as high as heaven, and God has remembered her iniquities." (Revelation 18:4-5) God was answering my heart's cry, but in a way I never imagined.

---

* Eight years later—after God had really worked these spiritual truths into my innermost being—I wrote the book, *Break Free from the Lusts of this World.* Although *At the Altar of Sexual Idolatry* has been the book most frequently associated with my name, I feel that *Break Free* is the most important book I have written. The spiritual implications conveyed in it have profoundly affected the lives of many people who have read it. For instance, Bob Gresh (*Who Moved the Goalpost?*, Moody Press) read it and exclaimed, "Steve, this isn't a book, it's a prophecy!" Kathy's sister, Linda, told her, "The message of this book is so important that I'm going to read it and keep reading it until it gets into me!"

These experiences created such an enthusiasm in me for the things of God that I would excitedly tell other ministers about the Faith Homes. I was amazed at the lack of interest. Others were sure that they had been to similar places: "Oh, yeah, I've been to a retreat center like that!" I couldn't seem to make people understand the depth and the riches of God's wisdom that flowed out of there. Eventually, I quit talking about the place and simply testified to what God had done in my life.

Every visit to the Faith Homes was like enjoying the breathtaking vistas of a mountain peak. On the other hand, life back at Pure Life was comparable to trudging through the quagmire of a murky swamp. No sooner would we arrive at home than financial crises, difficulties with hardhearted men, and even problems with our staff would beset us. However, the hardships of the jungle were simply opportunities for God to work into our beings the spiritual realities we were being presented at the Homes.

Little did we know that the upcoming New Year would present us with many such "opportunities."

---

[1] *The Pulpit Commentary*, Ezekiel 1, Ages Software.
[2] Zion Faith Homes, 2820 Eshcol Ave., Zion, IL 60099.
[3] ibid.

Thirteen

STAFF SHAKE UP

In January 1994, a Puerto Rican-Cuban from Long Island, NY arrived in the live-in program. Jeff Colón became involved in a life of drugs and promiscuity at an early age. What began as nothing more than recreational drug use soon developed into a serious habit. Inevitably, crime and violence came with this reckless lifestyle. Secretly, he began to develop a sexual addiction as well. There were times when he would spend entire nights in hotel rooms smoking crack and watching pornography. This quickly led to increasing encounters with prostitutes.

He met the Lord when he was 19 years old but continued abusing drugs and sleeping around. In 1991, he married a Christian girl named Rose. Things seemed to be coming together finally. He had gotten a good job as an elevator mechanic, and he and Rose started attending church together. However, Jeff was miserable inside and began disappearing for days at a time to pursue drugs and prostitutes. Finally, with pressure from his family and friends, Jeff admitted himself into Long Island Teen Challenge, an Assembly of God drug rehabilitation facility.

Jeff was a good student. He did all his homework, was obedient to his counselors, and successfully completed the program. But God wanted more than an outward surrender—He was after Jeff's heart. What needed to take place for him inwardly did not happen. Soon after he graduated, he fell back into drugs and sexual sin. Once again, he vanished, leaving Rose worried sick as he disappeared on another two-day binge. When he came back home this time, his pastor and wife confronted him. Rose was at the end of her rope. "You can't come home, Jeff. I've had it!"

Jeff's pastor, Jimmy Jack, suggested an alternative to going back into Teen Challenge. "Jeff, you can't come back to church anymore. You're a mess. What I suggest is that you go to Pure Life Ministries in Kentucky. They deal with sexual sin, and I think they can help you."

He was very angry about this ultimatum. He had become so hardened that he was ready to forget God and his whole Christian experience. And yet, as frustrated as he was, he was unwilling to completely turn his back on the Lord. Before the evening was over, he was on a bus headed to Kentucky.

Jeff didn't know what to expect at this obscure farm. He arrived at the bus depot to find Pete, our maintenance man, waiting for him. On the ride home, Pete told Jeff that few men return to their former lives after completing the program. Jeff did not know that this statement was untrue. A fear gripped his heart because he could not imagine living anywhere but New York; it was the only life he'd ever known. He tried to laugh off that statement, but deep in his heart he sensed that those words were prophetic. As they pulled onto the property, Jeff felt very much out of his comfort zone. He quickly made a decision to give God only six months (the length of his Pure Life commitment) to work in his life, or else! Or else, it would be back to the old, wild lifestyle in

"It didn't take me long to realize when I came to Pure Life that God was not playing games with me."

New York, without his wife and without God. This was it; one last shot at Christianity.

It did not take long for Jeff to realize that life at Pure Life was much different than anything he had ever experienced before. He could feel God's presence in a very real way. His outward behavior was de-emphasized, and more focus was given to the daily inward life. God began showing Jeff that He was looking for a true change in his heart. He would not allow him to simply conform to the rules of the program as he had done previously. The Lord began showing Jeff what a hypocrite he had been and challenged him to begin living what he claimed to believe. This self-confident electrician was being broken, one day at a time, one issue at a time.

"It didn't take me long to realize when I came to Pure Life that God was not playing games with me," Jeff recalled later. "He was calling me to get off the fence. I was either going to serve Him with all my heart as a real Christian, or I was going to completely give myself over to sin. The teachings at Pure Life were very clear about what it meant to be a disciple of Jesus Christ."

In the "dog-eat-dog" world of New York street life, Jeff had learned how to hate his enemies with all his heart. This deeply entrenched attitude was tested early in the program when he was forced to get along with a difficult roommate. Over time, Jeff began to despise him to the point that he couldn't even look at him. Nevertheless, wanting to obey God, he kept his feelings to himself. He did his best to tolerate the man. But the Lord hadn't commanded him to tolerate his enemy; he was expected to love him. Through this God revealed how unmerciful he was in his heart and urged him to pray for that man.

Jeff was at a real crossroads. It was clear to him that to go on with Jesus meant to love those around him—"all" those around him (without making exceptions). Every attempt at rationalization, every effort to sidestep this central issue, every endeavor to point the finger, left Jeff feeling hopelessly defeated. Criticizing the brother only caused Jeff to see his own glaring pride and high-mindedness. Jeff was in his own self-imposed prison and he knew it. He had to cry out to God for help, OR ELSE it was all over. He did the one thing Lance told him to do: he humbled himself and prayed earnestly for that brother.

At first, praying for him seemed ineffective and false. Jeff's words would just fall straight to the ground with no life in them whatsoever. Day after day, he would ask God to bless this brother and meet his needs with life-fulfilling mercies. Although he didn't feel anything, he was determined to do what he was taught at Pure Life. If it didn't work here, he was going to walk away from God and never come back.

One day while he was on "the prayer trail," Jeff saw his "enemy" through God's eyes. He began to break and weep in a true compassion for the man's soul. He knew what he was feeling was not from his own heart; it was God's heart breaking over the man's needs. Jeff was experiencing what the Lord goes through over hurting people everywhere, all the time.

But this was not all that happened inside him that day. Thoughts of the past flooded Jeff's mind. He remembered the tears of his loving wife, pleading with him to get help and surrender his life to Jesus. He remembered his pastor standing firm against his flesh and ordering him to go to Pure Life Ministries. These memories came crashing down

At that moment, he knew he <u>could</u> love this man, in fact, he knew he could love anybody.

upon him, and they all pointed to one word: MERCY! Suddenly, the tremendous mercy God had lavished upon him became very real. He fell in a heap before Him, overwhelmed with the magnitude of God's love for people and undone by how little love he had shown to others. He was broken like he had never been broken before. At that moment, he knew he *could* love this man, in fact, he knew he could love anybody. It was God's love flowing through his being!

This was a huge breakthrough in Jeff's life, but his real fork in the road was still ahead of him. Several months into the program, God had really begun to do a work in his heart. He was revealing His will to Jeff and made it clear to him that He expected him to live out *everything* he had been taught.

One evening, Lance told him that he might never return to New York. It was almost exactly what Pete had said when he first arrived at Pure Life. His whole being shook inside when he heard those words. The fear was so real that he literally felt cold. Jeff had always been an obsessive controller, but now the Lord was dealing with him about letting go of his own plans, letting go of the reins of his life. He shares what he experienced:

No matter how hard I tried to avoid or evade it, God kept pressing me about this issue in meetings, homework, counseling, and things I read in my Bible. God was tugging at my heart. I had been in the program for about five months when the Lord spoke very clearly to my inner man one day when I was out on the Ridge praying. "You are not going back to

your old life. I want you to leave all behind and serve
Me."

Oh, how I wrestled that day with God! I felt like
my whole insides were being torn to pieces. I knew
God was speaking to me. I knew if I didn't yield to
God's will, my life would be miserable and I would
be in trouble.

I wanted to live this consecrated life, but I wanted
to do it in New York, not Kentucky. I wanted it to fit
into my own life. But the Lord made it very clear to
me that day that there were two roads before me.
One was narrow and had no room for my own plans
or what was comfortable for me. The other was broad
and had plenty of room for what I wanted to do, my
life in New York, my career, my possessions and even
a little place for Jesus.

I finally gave in to God and chose the Narrow
Way. The minute I made the choice, all the pressure,
anxiety, and turmoil left and a peace that surpasses
all understanding came upon me. I immediately ran
up and called my wife. Victory, at last!

Unbeknownst to him, God was laying the same thing on
Rose's heart back in New York. It began as she was going
through *The Walk of Repentance*, a Bible study I had written
the year before:[1]

In *The Walk of Repentance*, there are historical
accounts of the lives of different Christians, such
as Hudson Taylor, Jonathan Goforth, Adoniram
Judson, Madam Guyon, etc. As I read these stories, I
began to see that these men and women of God had
something real in the Lord that enabled them to go

through the hardest of times, even to face death. They were living in a reality of the Lord that I knew I was lacking, and desperately wanted. God began stirring my heart to go after what these men and women of God had. It was then the Lord began calling me to come and live at PLM. I didn't know why, but the call was clear.

I prayed for about a month and said, "Lord if this is truly your will, lay it on my husband's heart." A couple of weeks later, Jeff called and told me that He wanted us to sell all we had and move to Kentucky. Needless to say when I got off the phone I jumped around praising the Lord because I was filled with such joy inside and had such great expectations. God was calling us out of what we had known and taking us into something deeper than we'd ever experienced!

It was good that God was bringing us new staff members because we were about to suffer the loss of the most important helper we had had since the beginning of the ministry. Lance had been a tremendous blessing in the lives of many men during the three years he had been counseling.

Unfortunately, he had some deeply held attitudes that had grown and festered within him during that period. Lance had always struggled with a judgmental spirit, but as time went on and he was given more responsibility and authority, he began to see himself above Kathy and me. A number of times he criticized us or treated us with disdain.

The problem was that working closely with us made him too familiar with us. On top of that, it was very easy for him to compare his own naturally quiet and gentler demeanor with my abrasive exterior. He became increasingly more self-righteous and conveyed the attitude that he was our superior. He was so consumed with the specks in our eyes that he became unwilling to see the beam in his own eye. Since he lost the capacity to see his own need, he became stuck spiritually and was no longer growing.

> *He slammed his fist onto our coffee table and stormed out of our house. We knew that the time had come for him to go.*

I knew something had to be done, but I hesitated. For my entire life, anytime I had relational problems with others, I always assumed that it was my fault. Steve Gallagher was the miserable wretch who couldn't get along with others. I knew Lance was right in many of his criticisms of me. How could I confront him about his attitude when I was such a mess myself? True, there was already a noticeable difference in me in the two years we had been involved with the Faith Homes. Yet, I still failed regularly. On top of all of that, Kathy and I sincerely loved Lance and didn't want to do anything that would further alienate him.

Over time, the tension grew between us until I was finally forced to confront him about his high-mindedness. After this he became more careful about how he handled himself outwardly, but inside, he remained essentially unbroken. He acknowledged the pride, but there was no visible evidence of heartfelt repentance. It all came to a head one day when he became enraged with Kathy and I over a cat we wanted to take to the pound. He slammed his fist onto our coffee table and stormed out of our house. When that happened, we knew inside that the time had come for him to go. With tears in my eyes, I told him he would have to leave Pure Life. The look of absolute astonishment on his face that day belied the fact that he considered himself as being indispensable and irreplaceable.

There are no words to express how brokenhearted Kathy and I both were over this. Nobody had been such an integral part of the family as Lance had. We considered Pure Life Ministries to be just as much his ministry as our own. And yet, I knew the Lord had prompted me to bring his time with us to a close. It was a loss we would feel for a long time to come.

———————

Meanwhile, I was suffering with another area of discouragement: my thought life. God had been doing such marvelous things within me through the experiences and teachings I received from the Faith Homes. I felt free inside like never before, and so I couldn't understand why I continued to struggle with the temptation to look at girls when out in public. I wanted to be completely and utterly free of any attraction to the opposite sex whatsoever, but when I would see girls wearing skimpy outfits, something in me still wanted to look at them—even to lust after them.

I had done everything I knew to overcome sexual lust. I had long since quit watching television, but I also fastidiously avoided places where scantily dressed girls would tend to be—beaches, malls, summer tourist spots, and so on. I pursued God and His holiness with all my heart. I did everything I knew to do to surrender to His workings in my life so that I might truly have "the mind of Christ" (Philippians 2:5) and "become a partaker of the divine nature." (II Peter 1:4) I pleaded with the Lord to purify my heart. In spite of all of this, when I went out in public, I was still very aware of the female anatomy and had to constantly deal with the urge to look.

I began to ask the Lord why this infatuation was still present within me. "Lord, is sexual sin an idol that I haven't surrendered to You? You know I do my best to control my eyes, but why do I still feel compelled to look at women?"

Over time, He began to give me deeper insight into this issue. The first truth that was revealed to me is that I still have a flesh nature.

> *There is an eternal value in resisting what comes so naturally to the fallen nature.*

True, Paul had said that if believers walk in the Spirit they would not fulfill the lusts of the flesh. (Galatians 5:16) However, He didn't say those lusts would go away, only that the believer would not act upon them. He taught me another important principle when I did a Bible study on the terms fight, battle, overcome, and violence. It became real to me that Christianity is meant to be a struggle. I realized that I was looking to avoid a battle that the Lord wanted me to be in. One day, I sensed the question arise within my spirit, "Steve, how can you be an overcomer if you have nothing to overcome?"

The more I considered the matter, the more convinced I became that I had been looking at the subject in the wrong way. There is an eternal value in resisting what comes so naturally to the fallen nature. Yes, my flesh is still drawn to women in a sexual manner, but God has called me to deny those carnal desires for His sake. I am to struggle against the desires of my flesh. I am a soldier of Christ and this is war. It is sheer cowardice to look to avoid the fight. Ultimately, I realized that God *had set me free.* I wasn't in sexual sin and I was doing my utmost to resist the temptation to indulge in sexual thoughts.

Over time, the Lord helped me to understand that He was doing a deep work within me. For now, I needed to focus upon Him and the men He sent to Pure Life for help. Those men needed someone who would love them and help them find freedom from the sin that had so powerfully overtaken them.

---

[1] Steve Gallagher, *The Walk of Repentance*, Pure Life Publishing.

Fourteen

TRIUMPHS AND TRAGEDIES

I first met Reggie Mieto while preaching at a church in the Boston area. He had grown up in the Fort Apache district of the Bronx in New York. This neighborhood is considered one of the most violent areas in the world. For this young, black Puerto Rican kid, there was no escaping the overwhelming sense of hopelessness that hovered like a cloud of foreboding darkness over the entire region. Nor was there any relief from a constant sense of fear. He never knew when older kids, or perhaps a gang, might attack him. He also never knew when guns would be drawn and bullets would fly in front of the bar on the corner. Growing up in such a precarious environment was all that Reggie had ever been exposed to—this was his life.

Rather than being sheltered from such harsh circumstances in a loving, nurturing home, young Reggie found life there to be as tough and chaotic as life on the streets. His domineering, schizophrenic grandmother, whom he was raised to believe was his mother, created a strife-filled environment in the home which resulted in a lot of bickering, backbiting, and even violence.

Life was difficult for Reggie, but when he was fourteen, a friend began teaching him how to play the drums. He was a natural. He could play for hours, lost in his own little world where there was no fear and no rejection. No one could hurt him there; he was safe and in control. Before long, he joined a band playing soul music in bars, clubs, dance halls and block parties. Eventually, he played in the Celebrity Club, one of the most prestigious black nightclubs in the country.

About that time, his grandmother decided to move back to Puerto Rico. Reggie was left to fend for himself on the streets. Many nights he would sleep on the subway train which traveled over to Coney Island and back, sometimes waking up to a car full of early morning commuters staring at him. Most of the time, however, he slept in the basement of a tenement building located nearby. As difficult as life was on the streets, anything was a welcome relief from living in the turbulent home he had grown up in.

Playing in the band gave Reggie a purpose in life—a sense of belonging. This was his only outlet. When he was fifteen, a music teacher befriended him and began to take a real interest in him. Reggie was excited to learn how to read music, how to make the most of his abilities. Most of all, someone really cared for him, but it wasn't long before he would come to realize that such affection had a price tag. The teacher was a homosexual pedophile who took advantage of the vulnerable young teen by seducing him into having sex with him. The troubled teen was not homosexually inclined, but consented in return for food, a warm bed, and the musical instruction he received. It was in the molester's home that Reggie was first exposed to the dark, seedy world of pornography.

One day, while his band was rehearsing, three young black men showed up to watch them play. They were an up-and-coming singing trio called the Delphonics. They liked what they heard and hired Reggie and his friends to play as their back-up band. The teenagers were ecstatic—they were in the "big league" now! Over the next couple of years they played in all the hottest clubs in New York. It wasn't uncommon for them to share the stage with singers like Al Green and groups like the Temptations or Cool and the Gang. Reggie was regularly backstage with the stars of the R & B music industry.

Life was beginning to deal this young man a decent hand for a change. It wasn't long before he was having the time of his life, dating beautiful girls, partying with popular entertainers, and snorting cocaine. Consequently, Reggie started becoming increasingly obsessed with sex and drugs. He had become well known in the black music world of New York and could land a job anywhere. Pretty soon, he was playing with ensembles and small orchestras in off-Broadway productions. Then, he got another break when he landed a job as drummer for Cab Calloway's Broadway musical, "Bubbling Brown Sugar." He then began to travel outside of New York and discovered an entire world he knew nothing about!

In 1981, at the age of twenty-four, he was hired to play in Roberta Flack's band. They traveled all over America and even to the Middle East. This was really the big time, staying in the finest hotels and arriving at concerts in chauffeured limousines. He didn't even have to set up his own drums; a road crew did everything for them!

Over the next several years, his cocaine addiction grew. He began borrowing money from other musicians, running up huge debts with his friends. As his addiction mounted, he also started ducking out of concerts during the breaks to get high, many times leaving the bewildered band to finish the set without a drummer. He simply failed to show up altogether at numerous other shows.

Reggie was in deep trouble. He went to therapy, read self-help books, and even turned to New Age teachings in his quest for the fulfillment in life that eluded him. On Halloween

One of the first things the Lord began to deal with me about at Pure Life was a deep-seated attitude that I was a victim in life.

night in 1987, he ran into a girl he had known from his schoolyard days who had become a Christian. She told him that the Lord could help him through a ministry called Teen Challenge in Brooklyn. That very night he took a subway to the same center which Doug and Millie had worked at years before. For the next eighteen months, Reggie stayed within the confines of Teen Challenge until he kicked his cocaine habit.

Unfortunately, his problems with sexual sin continued. In September of 1994, he enrolled in the Pure Life live-in program. Although the Teen Challenge program had played a major role in his life, establishing God's authority and learning self-discipline, the deeper issues of his heart had not yet been dealt with. Reggie recounts his early days at PLM:

> One of the first things the Lord began to deal with me about at Pure Life was a deep-seated attitude that I was a victim in life and, therefore, was not to be held responsible for my behavior. Somewhere along the line, I had come to understand what a poor upbringing I had. I began to see myself as a victim. Self-pity became an excuse for anything I wanted to do. It kept me from accepting responsibility for my actions in life. While I was at Pure Life, God made it very real to me that I was no longer a victim, but had, in fact, become a victimizer. I was destroying

> *Yes, God loved me greatly, but what also became very real to me at PLM was that God is not mocked.*

lives, just as others had done to me. I used other people without any concern for them whatsoever. The only person I cared about was myself.

The picture God showed me of what I was really like was horrible. I knew I needed to change.

The Lord also began to show me how I had created a false image of Him. I vacillated between two extremes. One day I saw Him as a loving God, but I just used this as an excuse to give over to my sin. "If He's so full of grace, surely He understands my struggles." Then, the next day, after I had plunged myself into sin again, I would make Him out to be an angry, vengeful tyrant who was looking to pour out His wrath on me. I could never seem to find the right balance.

I could see that the leaders at Pure Life had a fresh and real experience with God. It showed in their lives. I started to realize that God was not the angry tyrant I had made Him out to be. He was not sick and tired of me and my failures. He really did love me and desperately wanted to help me. I saw the gravity and ugliness of my sin and how flippant I had been about it in the past. Yes, God loved me greatly, that I came to understand, but what also became very real to me at PLM was that God is not mocked.

I came to a crossroads where I had to decide if I was going to repent of my selfish lifestyle and live the mercy to others that God had shown me or retreat back into self-pity and refuse to face what I was like. My stay at Pure Life was the hardest time

of my life. There were times the pain seemed unbearable, but I couldn't go on being a hypocrite. In
the end, I knew what I saw there was real and I had
to face the music. If I didn't respond to God, I would
end up dying.

Reggie graduated the program in the spring of 1995. He
moved to the Boston area and began working in a state-
funded home for troubled children. It was a wonderful opportunity for him to pour into others the love which God
had lavished upon him.

Several years later, Kathy and I visited with Reggie and
his new wife. We could hardly believe it was the same troubled
man who had gone through the live-in program! He had always seemed so fragile inside, but now there was a solidness
in his character that was not there before. Something was
completely different. He had finally "faced the music" and
now had a new life to show for it.

———•◦•———

By the time Reggie graduated, the ministry had been located at the new property on Fairview for three years. Pete
(our maintenance man), myself, and a couple of other guys
had built a number of buildings during that time. The motor
home Kathy and I used to travel the country back in 1989
had become Lance's home. When he left it remained vacant
for several months. One day, Pete suggested that we take the
camper section off the chassis. "That way, we can make a
flatbed out of the truck and use the camper shell for stor-
age," he offered. Kathy and I were both dubious about the
idea. Pete continued to persist and we finally acquiesced.

True to his word, he detached the camper from the chassis, jacked it up and drove the truck out from under it. The

Suddenly the jacks gave way and the camper crushed Pete underneath it.

camper section was sitting there on four jacks, and Pete began to block it up. I came out of the office one day to discover him lying under the camper working on it, as it was held up by nothing more than four flimsy jacks. I told him to come out from under it. "I'm almost done," he replied.

"Pete," I said firmly, "that is very dangerous. I want you to come out of there now!"

"I will, I will," he promised. Pete could be very stubborn and I certainly couldn't make him crawl out from under it, but I was very concerned. Later that day, I told him not to go back under that motor home. He half-heartedly agreed.

One of Pete's most pronounced struggles was a deep-seated strain of self-pity. He did not mind getting hurt if it meant gaining sympathy. It might sound like an innocent attitude, but—as is the case with any form of self-centeredness—it inevitably affects the lives of others. For instance, some months earlier, while driving on a winding road, he inadvertently crossed the line, almost hitting a car with a woman and her children. I told him he needed to be more careful. "It doesn't matter if I die," he lamented.

"Maybe it doesn't matter if *you* die, but what about that car full of kids!" I exclaimed. Pete carried around that "poor me" attitude everywhere he went in life. In some ways, it made him a danger to himself and others.

Two days after I told him not to climb back under the camper, he went right back and did it anyway. Suddenly the jacks gave way and the camper crushed Pete underneath it. A student and the wife of another guy in the program were the first ones on the scene. The woman bravely crawled under the motor home and dug the dirt out of Pete's mouth so he could breath. In the meantime, the student created a makeshift lever with a beam and somehow pried the motor home up just enough for her to pull Pete out. He wasn't breathing when they got him out, but they were able to resuscitate him. It was an incredible lifesaving feat on their part.

Someone else called the rescue squad who airlifted him to a hospital in Cincinnati. They immediately performed surgery on him to repair a crushed hip and pelvis. He was in I.C.U. for a few days and was released from the hospital a month later. Kathy visited him nearly every day during his stay; the rest of us on staff went to see him as often as we could.

The night he came home, he began complaining about feeling nauseous. Kathy drove him back to the hospital and got stuck in a traffic jam. He was getting increasingly worse as they sat in a long line of cars on the freeway. She did not realize that his bowel was perforated and he nearly died in the car. Once again the doctors performed lifesaving surgery on him.

A few days later he moved into our home where Kathy could tend to him. Over the next three months she nursed him back to health. In the meantime, Pete's medical bills were accumulating into tens of thousands of dollars. In my ignorance about such matters, I had never purchased worker's compensation insurance for the ministry. On his behalf, Kathy began the process of seeking Social Security aid to help pay for the bills, but Pete decided that he didn't want to accept governmental aid. We tried to explain to him that it was available for such situations, but his pride would not allow him to receive help from others.

In some ways, Pete was very difficult to care for. Kathy really did live out the love of God to him, but after awhile it became obvious that he was taking advantage of it. A number of things happened and one day he and I exchanged angry words. Although I repented over my part in the disagreement, Pete couldn't forgive me. So he left the ministry—full of self-pity—under the premise of seeking a better paying job so that he might pay his medical bills. The entire episode was tragic in every way. Once again, Kathy and I had to face the departure of a loved one on less than positive terms.

Fifteen

BROWNSVILLE

In June of 1996—for a variety of reasons—Doug and Millie retired from the Faith Homes where they had lived and ministered for over 30 years. The Faith Homes would never be the same again. The powerful spiritual climate that had been there for nearly the entire century greatly dissipated after their departure. The positive side to this was that Kathy and I became much closer to them. Doug eventually began a small ministry and asked me to serve as the vice president of the board of directors. He and Millie continued to come down to PLM to minister to the men. Our staff also visited them at their new home in Wisconsin in the same way we used to go to the Faith Homes.

Kurt and Michelle Koeshall had been trainees in the Homes for a year but left at the same time as Doug and Millie. They eventually came on staff at Pure Life. As a condition to being hired, Kurt asked me to take him down to Pensacola, Florida where a revival was taking place at Brownsville Assembly of God church.

I was hesitant to do this because it reminded me of the meetings that were taking place in a charismatic church in

Toronto. Having heard bizarre stories about things occurring in the Toronto church (such as people barking like dogs) left me highly skeptical of Brownsville. "The last thing America needs right now is another sideshow!" I exclaimed.

He asked me to watch a video of Steve Hill, a missionary evangelist who was holding the meetings there at Brownsville. The entire staff gathered around a television set one night to see his preaching. I was greatly relieved to hear him deliver a very strong message about the need for Christians to repent of worldliness and sin and to get their lives right with God. I still had my reservations, but after watching the video, I agreed to take Kurt down there. We were scheduled to leave the following Tuesday.

That Saturday, Kathy and I decided to drive to a Christian bookstore in Cincinnati. We weren't doing anything but killing time (this outing was a big event for people who don't watch television!) and looking at various books. I picked up a Bible and opened it randomly to Isaiah 42. I certainly wasn't looking for anything—I was simply checking out the layout of this particular Bible. However, my eyes fell on verse 6:

> "I am the LORD, I have called you in righteousness, I will also hold you by the hand and watch over you, and I will appoint you… to open blind eyes, to bring out prisoners from the dungeon, and those who dwell in darkness from the prison... Behold, the former things have come to pass, now I declare new things; before they spring forth I proclaim them to you."

When I read that passage, the words pierced my heart like an arrow. It was clearly a direct word from the Lord to me. I showed the passage to Kathy and she experienced the same thing! We had no idea what it meant to our lives. Nevertheless, there was simply no questioning the fact that God was saying *something* to us.

A surge of power went through me, and I crumpled to the floor.

Kurt and I made the long trip down to Pensacola the following Tuesday. People were so excited about the meetings that the lines began forming in front of the church early in the morning. Thousands of people were there by the time the evening service began. The sanctuary only seated 2,000 so the rest had to watch the service on big projector screens in other buildings.

That evening Steve Hill preached about the backslidden condition of the Church. Hundreds of people came streaming forward when he invited them to come down to the altar to repent. Some were visibly broken, as they cried out to the Lord for mercy.

Once the altar time finished, the team of ministers walked out into the crowd laying hands on people. Folks were falling over as soon as the ministers touched them—sometimes they never even made contact with people.

As I stood in the crowd, one of the pastors came by and touched my stomach. A surge of power went through me, and I crumpled to the floor. It left me in a state of exhilaration that lasted all night. In fact, when I got in bed at the motel, I couldn't sleep. All night long wave after wave of liquid love (I can't think of any better description) flowed through me. I was full of so much joy that I could hardly contain it.

It reminds me of an experience that happened to Dwight Moody. He had been seeking God for a greater infilling of the Holy Spirit. "Well, one day," he recounted later, "in the city of New York—oh, what a day!—I cannot describe it. I seldom refer to it; it is almost too sacred an experience to name. I can only say that God revealed Himself to me, and I had to ask Him to stay His hand."[1]

Kurt and I returned to Kentucky with a renewed love for God. To our amazement, it gradually became clear to Kathy and me that the Lord wanted us to move to Pensacola. The more we prayed about it, the clearer the message became. We moved there February 1, 1997, just as the revival was hitting its peak. We stayed involved with Pure Life over the phone, but we put the day-to-day operations in the hands of Jeff and Rose Colón.

After seven years of living with troubled men in all kinds of sexual sin—24 hours a day, 7 days a week—it was a wonderful respite to be able to live like "normal" people for awhile. It had been hard on both of us, dealing with these men over the years, but I didn't realize how difficult it had been for Kathy.

Not long after we arrived in Florida, Jeff and Rose came for a visit. Kathy shared with Rose how she had struggled for so long feeling sexually unclean, not because of things she had done in the past, but because she was often harassed by men in public. Although she dressed modestly, she felt like she was doing something to provoke these verbal assaults. She poured her heart out to Rose about it, and they both prayed for God's help. It seemed that the enemy was targeting her because of the nature of our ministry.

Suddenly Pastor John Kilpatrick appeared. He fixed his eyes on Kathy and started to move toward her.

That night, after the altar time, Kathy and I stood along the side wall of the sanctuary, watching the ministers move through the throngs of people. Suddenly Pastor John Kilpatrick appeared. He fixed his eyes on Kathy and started to move toward her. Amazingly, the power of God emanating from his body caused her to stumble backward as he approached. He finally caught up to her and put his hands on her head. He prayed a prayer that exactly described what Kathy and Rose had been discussing. As he prayed, Kathy felt like a black cloud lifted off her. The sense of dirtiness vanished as well. She felt clean and free for the first time in years.

However, the effects of the revival were not just felt while in the meetings. Kathy's prayer times also became dramatically affected. One morning, while I was out on my customary prayer walk, she was listening to some *Vineyard* music, worshipping God. She describes what happened:

> All of the sudden I knew that Jesus was in the room. Instantly I fell on my face and began weeping uncontrollably. He was so near to me it was almost like He was touching me. I just stayed on the floor. I would try to get up but couldn't. For the next two or three weeks, every time I went into that room in the morning, He was there waiting for me, His love filling the atmosphere. During those encounters I felt strongly compelled to pray for my husband. I would go into very intense intercession for Steve. There were times when I simply knew it was the Holy Spirit praying through me on my husband's behalf.
>
> I couldn't wait for Steve to leave in the mornings so I could meet with God. One morning, Steve had just left and I went into the living room and I couldn't feel God's presence. I was heartbroken and upset. I felt like He had abandoned me. Looking back, I now understand that it was only meant to be for a period

of time. I think He was giving me a taste of what I had to look forward to when He returns.

We were wonderfully blessed in many ways during those months in Pensacola.* One day, Jeff called from home. "Steve, I have some bad news. We just received a notice from the State of Kentucky. Pete has filed a claim with the Workers Compensation Board. He's suing Pure Life for his medical bills." We were devastated. I could see no way we would be able to come up with all of the money that would be needed to pay those bills. "He could also sue us for the loss of future wages," I lamented to Kathy. "In fact, this lawsuit could end up being over a million dollars!"

Somehow we made it to the meeting that evening. At the close of the service, the ministers began praying for different ones throughout the sanctuary. We were still in a state of shock and had no desire to be prayed for. We were stand-

---

* Some people have asked about similarities between the Faith Homes and the Brownsville revival. I felt the same crisp, refreshing sense of God's presence in Pensacola as I did in the Homes. I *knew* that He was there. The way God dealt with people in each place was much different, however. At Brownsville, He moved in an outward way. People were healed, miracles occurred and Christians were "slain in the Spirit." Furthermore, there was a very real conviction over outward sins such as drug abuse, sexual promiscuity, and being backslidden. Steve Hill preached with fire, but his messages were simple and tended to deal with surface issues. His preaching was primarily aimed at unsaved youth and backslidden Christians. I should also mention that the revival attracted many "super-spiritual" types who didn't seem nearly as interested in finding God as they were in experiencing some new spiritual sensation.

The ministry that occurred at the Faith Homes was on a much deeper level. The depth of truth being offered there was nothing less than astounding. There was a very rich and profound comprehension of the spiritual realm that exposed sins buried deeply within a person's heart. The ministry that went on there was not geared toward the backslidden but those who were hungry to know God in a much greater way. There was nothing for the flesh at the Faith Homes; only a great reality of God. We were encouraged by our time at Brownsville, but we could never compare what happened for us there with what occurred in our lives at the Faith Homes.

ing by a pew when Pastor Kilpatrick suddenly appeared. He began making his way through the crowd toward us. "The devil's try-

> *"The devil's trying to put something on you, brother," he said.*

ing to put something on you, brother," he said. With that, he simply laid his hands on our heads and moved off to other people. As soon as his hand touched our heads, the overwhelming dark cloud that had enveloped us was instantly gone. For the next six months, until the case was settled, Kathy and I never had one more fearful thought about it. We *knew* God was going to take care of it. In fact, we were so confident about the outcome, we had to force ourselves to pray about it!

In August we began to sense that our time at Brownsville was coming to an end. I was very anxious to go out preaching as an evangelist—thinking it to be the "new thing" that God had promised for my life. He hadn't released us from Pure Life, but we were ready to walk away from it if and when He directed us to. We booked nearly three months of services in churches in New England for that fall. However, before we left for the Northeast, a couple of churches in Wisconsin invited me to preach.

I was excited and anxious to minister in churches. I had heard the stories of a number of evangelists who had gone out from Pensacola with the same power that was evident in Brownsville. I fully expected the same to be the case when I preached but was tremendously disappointed when nothing visible happened. People felt convicted about their sin and repented, but there was no dramatic sense of God's presence sweeping them off their feet.

I was very dejected when we paid a visit to Doug and Millie's house in Wisconsin. Being with them was such an

I didn't understand it at the time, but God was promising to give me something better than the power to make people fall down.

encouragement as I reflected upon all of the wonderful things the Lord had done for us at the Faith Homes. Seeking the Lord at their house was much like it had been at the Homes. One morning, I haphazardly opened my Bible to the book of Proverbs. My eyes fell on the following words: "How blessed is the man who finds wisdom, and the man who gains understanding. For its profit is better than the profit of silver, and its gain than fine gold. She is more precious than jewels; and *nothing you desire compares with her.*" (Proverbs 3:13-15)

I had the same undeniable sense that God was speaking to me as I had when I read the Isaiah passage. I didn't understand it at the time, but God was promising to give me something better than the power to make people fall down. He was giving me an insight into spiritual matters that would be worth far more than what I longed for. At the time, I am ashamed to say, this passage was very little comfort to me. I wanted spectacular results from my preaching and was very disappointed that I wasn't getting them.

Kathy and I purchased a 22-foot travel trailer and towed it to New England, setting it up at a state park on the beach. That would be our home that fall during our stay. On weekends we would travel to churches all over New England, spending the weekdays in our trailer. It was a wonderful time for both of us. Since we were parked near the beach, I was able to take prayer walks along the seashore—usually watching the sun as it rose over the Atlantic Ocean.

One weekend, we had to travel to a small Assembly of God church in Vermont. I preached a hard-hitting message that Sunday morning. People responded to the invitation and were on their knees praying, crying and seeking God. Kathy was sitting on the front row and I went to sit next to her. She had been watching this young man named Bart—who had obvious Mongoloid features—walk around apparently praying for people at the altar. In her heart, she was cringing at the thought of him coming up to her. There was something about him that was repulsive to her. Suddenly—as she was watching him—she realized it wasn't Bart; it was Jesus praying for others through him! Full of shame over her prideful attitude, Kathy buried her head in her hands and started weeping over the ugliness of her pride.

I didn't know what was going on inside her and just continued to sit there, a little worn out from preaching. All of the sudden Bart came up beside me and awkwardly put his arm around my head. He was only there for a moment, but in that one instant, I experienced the love of God like never before. This was different than the Brownsville encounter. Deep in my heart I knew that this man hugging me could not possibly have one single critical thought about me. Having been raised in a home where I was constantly criticized had caused me to fear people's judgmental thoughts. But in that one split-second, I knew what it was like to be loved by God.

When he walked by Kathy without hugging her, she began sobbing uncontrollably. She felt as though Jesus had passed her by because of her pride. Then, all of a sudden, Bart was back! He hugged her head in the same awkward manner in which he had embraced me. Now she really fell apart! As she convulsed in tears, he patted her on the back and said, "It's otay." She knew that it was God communicating His love to her.

We finished out our stay in New England and eventually returned home. When we arrived at Pure Life, we discovered that Jimmy Jack—the minister who had sent Jeff to Pure Life earlier—had sent a black man named George Mooney to us. George looked like he was on death's door when he arrived. He was dying of AIDS.

George had grown up in a ghetto area of New York and spent his teenage years pursuing drugs and sex. His mother died while he was in the Army, and after that, he completely gave himself over to a sinful lifestyle. By the time he left the military in 1982, he had become a full-fledged heroin addict.

Nothing became too shameless for George. Sometimes he would spend all night roaming the Times Square District of Manhattan, bouncing from adult bookstores to strip clubs to massage parlors, in his pursuit of illicit sex. At the same time, his heroin use had increased to an alarming $100-a-day habit. He ended up living on the streets of New York, doing anything he could to survive, including stealing and eating out of garbage cans. He spent most nights sleeping on a ratty mattress in a high-rise, outdoor parking garage. Now fully engrossed in the street life, it was not uncommon for George to see friends shot or stabbed.

When it seemed as though he could not possibly sink any lower, George ran into an old acquaintance from his teenage drug days, Jimmy Jack who had sent Jeff to PLM in 1994. Jimmy had gotten wonderfully saved and delivered from drug abuse and now directed a Teen Challenge Drug Rehabilitation Center on Long Island. For the first time in his life, George saw his great need to change. He entered the Teen Challenge Center in 1990 and graduated the following year. Upon graduation, he became a staff member; however, his problems were far from over.

Although Teen Challenge had helped him overcome his

drug habit, he had never dealt with his sexual addiction. While secretly involved with pornography and sometimes even frequenting prostitutes, George's spiritual life ebbed

> *If there was one thing George knew, it was that he had no intention of going to some strange ministry in the "boonies" of Kentucky.*

away. For the next five years, George's life was a roller-coaster ride which took him back and forth from the Teen Challenge program to the street life. It was during this time that he contracted the HIV virus. Thankfully, in January 1997, Jimmy Jack confronted him and gave him two options: he could either go to Pure Life Ministries or he could return to the streets. If there was one thing George knew, it was that he had no intention of going to some strange ministry in the "boonies" of Kentucky. He returned to his old stomping grounds—the streets. Because of his stubbornness, he went back to wallow in the pigpen once more.

Finally, after more degradation he gave up. Almost lifeless, he ran to his pastor in desperation. "Jimmy, I'll do anything. I need help!"

"Are you willing to go to Kentucky, George?" Jimmy asked.

"Yes, I am willing," George mumbled.

In November of 1997, George Mooney dragged himself into the Pure Life Ministries live-in program half-dead. Years of drug addiction on the streets of New York, in addition to his being HIV positive, had brought him very close to the point of death. Barely willing and barely alive, George showed up grossly underweight. Coming to Pure Life was his last shot at life—his last opportunity to find Jesus. The staff saw how bleak his situation was and knew nothing short of a miracle could save this poor man.

> *God knew what it would take to finally get my undivided attention, and He brought me to a place where I realized He was my only hope.*

He soon discovered that his real problem was neither drug addiction nor sexual addiction. It was his unwillingness to fully surrender to God. This came to light in a most unexpected way. George had always been a master at "working the system." He knew how to scheme to get his way. He did this with governmental agencies and with the various Christian leaders who had tried to help him. Using a bubbly smile and an adorable personality, he always managed to work angles to get his way. What he did not realize was that God was bringing him to a place in his life where he would have to make a decision about what he wanted. This started to come about as the Lord exposed him for who he really was. As George explains:

> God knew what it would take to finally get my undivided attention, and He brought me to a place where I realized that He was my only hope. While I was going through the program, I discovered that I had no love for anybody except myself. I would go to my counselor and complain about others. I would always point the finger to expose how "messed up" they were, not seeing my own arrogant, prideful and critical heart. I was extremely unmerciful. God started revealing to me through His word how I was unlike Him. My outward mask was ripped off and the real me was exposed, as God started changing my inside world. As I read verse 7 of the "Love Chapter" (I Corinthians 13) "... love beareth all things...," my heart

broke. How could this King of kings love me like this while I was unwilling to bear anyone who did not meet my standards? His love was becoming real to me.

God was softening his heart, but George was still maneuvering to get his way. While the state of New York is very liberal in its benefits for the needy, Kentucky, on the other hand, tends to be more conservative in the area of social services. Knowing "the system" in New York, George had arranged to receive an on-going prescription to help combat the effects of the AIDS virus. He attempted to get this prescription in Kentucky but was unfortunately denied. The wheels were already turning in his mind as he sought to take matters into his own hands:

It was obvious I would have to return to New York to arrange to get my prescription sent to Kentucky. I talked it over with Jeff Colón, the director of the live-in program. He agreed that it seemed to be the only solution to my problem. "Just clear it with Steve. It should be no problem," Jeff told me. What I didn't tell Jeff, and I'm not sure that I was admitting to myself, was that my real plan, once I got back to New York, was to scheme my way back into Teen Challenge. I wanted out of Kentucky in a big way, partially because I was used to the city life, and also because all my friends were there. But most importantly, it was because God was squeezing me at Pure Life and I was looking for a way of escape—out of the "fire."

After talking with Jeff, I approached Steve one day as he was passing through the men's home. I quickly explained the situation to him, the need to temporarily return to New York to get my medication. I thought it was the obvious thing to do. I was shocked when Steve simply said, "George, you're not going to New York. You've got to trust the Lord." With that simple statement, he just walked out of the room, leaving me there with my mouth hanging open.

My first reaction was anger. "How could he just blow me off like that?! Doesn't he realize it's my life at stake here?" On and on, I railed against him in my mind. I went out to the "prayer trail" to have it out with God. I wasn't used to not getting my way. I finally calmed down and began to pray. All I could hear was his final statement: "You've got to trust the Lord... You've got to trust the Lord." Over and over, it played in my mind. I realized it was God speaking to me. For the first time in my life, I made the decision to trust God rather than my own abilities. "God, You're right. I've always trusted in my abilities to get things done. This time I'm going to give You a chance. I really am going to trust You this time. I can't afford to leave this place without you Lord, so You're going to have to provide for the medication." As I made this resolution to trust God, I was at peace for the first time since I had gotten there.

The very next day, someone told George that the VA covers medication for veterans who are HIV positive. He qualified and got his medication for free! The whole incident was a wonderful lesson in trusting God.

With that experience behind him, George began to put his heart into the program. Instead of simply doing the outward things just to be noticed by man, it became real to him that the live-in program was a contract between himself and the Lord. When he graduated from the program, he was invited to become a ministry intern. He spent the next nine months in training. When one of the Pure Life ministers accepted the call of God to another ministry, George was invited to come on staff as a counselor. God would use him in many men's lives over the years to come.

[1] James Gilchrest Lawson, *Deeper Experiences of Famous Christians*, The Warner Press, Anderson, IN, 1911, p. 247.

Sixteen

CHANGED LIVES!

ot long after this happened, a young man named Justin Carabello came to Pure Life from his home in Reading, Pennsylvania. Justin was a very successful junior high school band director. He didn't take drugs and was physically fit, but he was a shambles spiritually. Although he had been raised in Pentecostal churches, he was a complete fraud. Outwardly affable, with an uncanny ability to present a godly image to those around him, in secret he was obsessed with sex. His pastor sent him to us when his wife caught him going to a prostitute. It also came out that he had been embezzling funds from a special band account to fund his extra-curricular activities.

Justin came to Pure Life unbroken and unrepentant over his sin. He was hardened and bitter towards his wife because she decided to divorce him. Even as he was preparing to leave for Kentucky, he was involved in an adulterous relationship with the eighteen-year-old sister of one of his former students. He drove into PLM as far from God as a person can be. However, the spiritual atmosphere there quickly affected him. "When I entered the live-in program," he later recounted, "I encountered a depth of Christianity in the staff that was unfamiliar to me. Their words had the power to make me believe I could truly know Him. It was obvious that sin did not hold them, and I wanted what they had."

The first thing Jeff told him to do when he arrived was to establish a daily devotional time. He told him to pray at least thirty minutes and read two to three chapters of the Bible everyday. He was also expected to do his daily homework in *The Walk of Repentance.* The hardest thing he was asked to do was to pray for his wife. He wanted to remain cold towards her, but he honored his commitment and reluctantly did what he was told. She eventually divorced him, but God made his heart right toward her through his prayers.

At first, Justin approached everything very studiously. His answers to the homework were simply out of the wealth of "head knowledge" he had accumulated over twenty-six years of going to church. His prayers were dry and full of self. He was doing the only thing he knew how to do—fake religion. Then one Sunday morning in a service, about three weeks after his arrival, Jeff confronted him about being a "Pharisee." He said that if he didn't let God change him, he would never grow close to Him. Justin knew what Jeff had said was true; so he got alone with God and told Him that he didn't want to be a Pharisee. He sincerely asked Him to humble him and to show him who he really was. God was faithful to honor Justin's prayer by revealing to him what Jesus is like through the Scriptures and by putting a hunger in him to be more like Him. He slowly started to see his need to repent and come to the Cross—a place he had always avoided in the past.

God began to draw Justin very close to Himself. This was a new experience for this young hypocrite! He had never experienced the presence of God like this before. As he began to see what the Lord is like, he also became increasingly aware of his own pride, covetousness, selfishness, and contempt for other people. Many nights he spent out on the "prayer trail" agonizing over his pride and selfishness. Gradually his perspectives about other people began to change. He had always been so wrapped up in himself that he had never had an interest in anybody else. It was like he was coming out of a cocoon and seeing people in a whole new light. For the first time in his life, he sincerely began praying for other people—their problems, needs, and concerns. Sexual sin completely lost its hold on his life as he was changed from the inside out.

Justin's initial plan upon arriving at Pure Life was to complete the program and return to Pennsylvania to resurrect his teaching career. As he drew closer to God, his thoughts became focused on how the Lord could use him as a music teacher. He considered every conceivable alternative. The painful truth, which he did not want to see, was that, although he had certainly had a breakthrough, *he* was still in the center of all of his plans.

He was anxious to put the Pure Life experience behind him and to get on with his life. And yet, every time he thought in terms of what he wanted to do, he felt a "check in his spirit." The problem was that, in spite of the nagging sense that God had other plans, Justin was determined to regain control of his life. For the next month, he agonized nightly on the ridge behind the office building in prayer, many times to the point of deep sobbing. The anguish he was experiencing was because it was obvious what God was after—his life. But he was resisting the call. The Lord was calling Justin to sit at His feet, to know Him, and to love Him. But Justin loved his own life more and was not willing to give it up— not even for Him. He describes his struggle:

Eventually I could not set my mind to pray without facing this decision. What was I going to do? Would I forsake all and follow Jesus—not knowing

God had backed me into a corner and was demanding that I choose between having Him and having my own life.

where that was leading me, or would I settle for a mediocre relationship with Jesus at best and do what I wanted to do? I knew that, as far as the Christian world was concerned, I was completely justified to think that I could have my cake and eat it too. Yet, at the same time, I was learning to see the hideous sin behind that self-centered way of thinking.

Gradually, the Lord helped me see that there was never going to be true lasting peace in my life until I surrendered what I wanted to do. My all was not yet on the altar. This was so very difficult for me to accept. I so much wanted there to be a compromise— to be able to strike a deal with the Lord. In those times of prayer, I made every conceivable offer to the Lord I could think of. His answer remained the same to all of them, "You need to know Me."

God had backed me into a corner and was demanding that I choose between having Him and having my own life. I remember the evening I made my decision very well. It was a Thursday night, during a meeting at PLM, and the Lord was there in a special way. The meeting ended that particular evening with a staff member encouraging the men to give Jesus everything. He invited the men to come to the altar to pray. I fell in a heap at the foot of the piano and told the Lord He could have everything: my life, my

> *Once Justin had allowed the Lord to break through, he began to really fall in love with Him.*

music, my career, my marriage—He could have it all in exchange for Himself. I had never imagined those words would come out of my mouth and that I could really mean such things. I knew that God had finally won my heart. I walked out of that chapel heading down the way of the Cross for the first time in my life. I had laid down my life in this world for Him. Never have I known such peace and satisfaction in making a decision.

Once Justin had allowed the Lord to break through, he began to really fall in love with Him. As he focused on reading through the gospels after that, he would sit in wonder and amazement at the things Jesus said. "How had I missed the life in those words all these years," he wondered. He began communing with the Lord in his heart throughout the day. One night, he was lying out under the stars talking to the Lord. At one point in the conversation he rolled over onto his side and the sense that Jesus was right there with him was overwhelming. The innocence of God's love gripped him, making him feel unbelievably pure inside. He melted into a heap of tears. He had never experienced feeling anything like this before. His whole desire became to please the Lord in every way.

It became clear to the staff that God was calling Justin to be a part of Pure Life Ministries. In March of 1999, he entered the PLM Intern Program. He graduated eight months later and was asked to come on staff. He had made his choice, one night at the foot of the piano. His life was not his own, for he had offered his life on the altar.

Meanwhile, the time had come to settle the case with Pete. The only thing that matters with worker's compensation cases is whether or not the man was working for the organization when the accident occurred. The concept of right and wrong or who is at fault plays no part in the settlement process. Pete was working for Pure Life Ministries when the accident occurred, and there was nothing we could do to defend ourselves. We were completely at the mercy of the state arbitrator.

The hearing took place at our attorney's office. Also present was the man who was representing the State of Kentucky. The five of us—the arbitrator, the state representative, our attorney, Kathy and I—sat around the conference table. The state representative had already told our attorney in a previous conversation that he expected us to pay the entire $100,000 in medical bills—a figure that was actually a relief to us, as we had feared that it could be a much greater sum. To his credit, Pete didn't "go after us." He simply wanted to pay his bills and cover the hip-replacement surgery he still needed. We didn't have the foggiest notion how we would get the money; we only knew that God had given us peace about the entire matter while we were in Pensacola. Nevertheless, the stern look on the bureaucrat's face confirmed the fact that he was not sympathetic to our cause.

The arbitrator laid out the essentials of the case and asked us if the information was correct. "Yes, that is what happened," I responded.

"Would you like to make a statement?" he asked.

"Yes sir, I would," I replied. With that, I explained the entire situation. I told them that we loved Pete and were very concerned about him. We wanted him to receive whatever medical attention he would need in the future. I also mentioned that I had told him twice to come out from under that camper shell, but he had refused. However, I understood that I was at fault for not providing worker's compensation insurance. I also briefly poured out my heart about the importance of the work we were doing for men at our ministry.

The man representing Kentucky was listening very intently to me. By the time I finished, his somber countenance had dissolved into one of compassion. "I came in here with the determination that your organization was going to pay the entire amount of these bills," he said. "However, after hearing what you have expressed, I would like to rescind our previous demand and make you an offer. The State of Kentucky will match dollar for dollar; if you will pay $50,000 toward these bills, we will cover the rest."

Kathy and I could hardly believe our ears! We left the hearing that day with the bill cut in half. We were extremely relieved, but we still had to come up with $50,000—and if we didn't, we would be held liable for the entire amount.

That day we brought the staff together to pray about it. A couple of days later, one of the counselors asked if he could speak to me in private. "Steve, you know that I saved up a lot of money over the years," he earnestly told me. "I feel like God is telling me that I have put my trust in my savings account instead of Him. I want to pay that $50,000." The Lord had not only given us a deep sense of peace throughout the entire ordeal but was faithful to take care of the entire amount that was due!

———◆———

In the meantime, God continued to change the lives of men at Pure Life Ministries. One such man was a serious young black man named Bradley Furges. He had become involved in homosexuality and crack cocaine while in college. He came to the Lord in 1991, but years of sin and rebellion followed. When he completed college, he entered medical school. Unfortunately, his

> *Brad was coming to an end of his rope. He knew he needed to do something. It was then that he found out about the live-in program.*

partying lifestyle took its toll upon his studies. He was eventually expelled.

By the summer of 1997, Brad was coming to an end of his rope. He knew he needed to do something. It was then that he found out about the live-in program. He soon arrived not knowing what to expect. He shares some of his first impressions:

> Because I only went there to deal with "my issues" (which centered only around my struggles with homosexuality), humbling myself to others or even being merciful to an undeserving individual were concepts foreign to me and of no great interest to me. However, as I began to read *At the Altar of Sexual Idolatry*, I was exposed. I got my first glimpse of how corrupt I was and how ignorant I was of the true character and nature of God despite the fact that I professed in my testimony which I sent in that "I love God." Page by page and chapter after chapter, I saw that I was guilty as charged—a sinner without excuse. Who was I to blame now? Could it really be true that I was responsible for all the sin and degradation I wallowed in for years? Nevertheless, I found hope... there was a way out that I did not quite understand yet.

Brad's will was crossed countless times in the months ahead. The Lord was trying to teach him that if he was ever going to escape from the prison of "self" he had lived in for so many years, he would have to learn to love other people and humble himself to them. The more he resisted this, the more miserable he became inside. The first four months of his time at Pure Life were characterized by getting angry and by having major conflicts with those around him. His critical, judgmental, unmerciful heart was continually exposed. This was not easy and yet, Brad knew that God's hand was in the process in a powerful way. Refusing to give up or lose hope, he continually cried out for help.

Just when it seemed as though he could not take another trial in life, he was forced to deal with his sexual lust. This had not been a real problem during the first few months of the program, but then another young black man showed up who was also out of the gay lifestyle. Brad shares his reflections on how this affected him:

> A man named Jake became my first struggle with overwhelming temptation and desire for the forbidden. The "wrestling match" between my flesh and God's Spirit commenced. God mercifully used my struggles with Jake to expose what was buried deep within my heart... a wicked, evil, disobedient, and rebellious nature that utterly refused to be denied access to something that was tantalizing or seemingly gratifying.
>
> *Rather than being a real blessing to him, I began to entertain lustful thoughts. I was treading dangerous territory, looking back at Sodom, so to speak.*
>
> Before long, after several unwholesome

conversations reminiscing about the "old days" of sin and insanity, Jake and I knew that we definitely came out of the same cesspool. Rather than being a real blessing to him, I began to entertain lustful thoughts. Yes, I was treading dangerous territory, looking back at Sodom, so to speak. Unbeknownst to me, my idolatrous feelings were slowly leading me back down the path of backsliding.

As much as they toyed with the thought of it, it is amazing that Brad and Jake didn't run away together. Several times, during that period, Jeff Colón was ready to ask them both to leave, but each time, he felt the Lord restrain him. In the meantime, the two of them continued to battle with overwhelming temptation. The staff couldn't see it at the time, but Brad was growing in strength through the whole ordeal. Just when it seemed as though he was going to make it through, he and Jake hugged each other inappropriately. He describes what he went through after this incident:

I was devastated. I felt like I had just smoked crack and was out of money. Totally empty. Full of guilt. Full of fear. All the next day, I repented and asked God to help me out of this once again. I was in such great despair because I knew that there was a good chance that I would get kicked out after being repeatedly warned over the last two months. The ridiculous thought came in my mind to consider moving to Cincinnati with Jake if we were asked to leave. Wait! Wait one minute! No way! I did not come all the way out here to not get what I came here for! What other ministry was out there to confront my sin and offer me hope and a way out of myself...

into Jesus Christ? I knew that the path that *seemed* right was not the answer.

Jake pleaded with me that morning not to tell, fearing that because I had gone to staff previously when we struggled that I would reveal our latest encounter. I knew that confession was the only way out. I could not have imagined going through the motions and not confessing it to staff. God is a God of Mercy at Pure Life, but He is also a God of Exposure too. Sin cannot hide there. So that evening after work, I told Jake we had to go to Steve Gallagher... "Steve Gallagher? You're crazy!" was his reply. Mr. Gallagher's serious devotion to God terrified us both. Nevertheless, I dragged Jake with me to see him. To my utter amazement, he did not rebuke us.

When Brad and Jake came to me I responded with compassion and tried to encourage them. "I can't imagine what it would be like if I were living in a place surrounded by women," I told them. But then, I suddenly felt a strong sense of sobriety come over me. I looked Bradley in the eye and told him firmly, "Stay away from Jake. Look at me." Pointing my finger right in his face I said, "You stay away from Jake."

"It was just what I needed," Bradley later recounted. Indeed, after that, he never struggled with that temptation again. From this point on, the two men were headed in different directions. It wasn't long after this incident that Jake was asked to leave because of his rebellious attitude. With Jake out of the picture, Brad really began to press into the Lord.

When he graduated the live-in program in December, he was invited to become an intern. Now his spiritual life wonderfully blossomed. Had he had a say in the matter, he would have avoided the overwhelming temptation which Jake's appearance presented. But the Lord knew exactly what he needed and what he could handle. Bradley made it through the fiery test and came out the other end as silver refined in the crucible.

Now he has a bountiful life in God. Instead of the gloomy, depressed person he used to be, he is a bubbling fountain of the joy of the Lord. He has become a vital part of the work which goes on at Pure Life Ministries—a work that would take some interesting turns in the days ahead.

Seventeen

A NEW THING

*S*omeone once said, "Nothing will ruin a friendship as quickly as traveling together." Jeff and I learned this firsthand when we took a one-month trip to Israel and Jordan during the month of March 1999. It was my third extended visit to the Middle East and Jeff's first. We were able to spend part of the time visiting the ancient sites, while the rest of our stay was spent preaching at Assembly of God churches in Amman, Jordan.

There are a number of reasons the above saying so often proves true. Traveling can be difficult. Rushing to meet buses or trains, staying in uncomfortable locations, and growing weary from lack of sleep all contribute to a poor attitude. On top of that, it is difficult to maintain a solid devotional life while running at such a frantic pace—often leaving the believer in a carnal mindset.

By the time we went on this trip together, Jeff and Rose had been working for Pure Life Ministries for nearly five years. We already had a deep camaraderie from the many spiritual battles we had been through together. Nevertheless, during our trip we allowed petty annoyances to grow, and we became increasingly irritated with each other. When we arrived back in the States, we could hardly wait to get away from one another.

Instead of things getting better back home, the tension between us mounted. One day, we decided to clear the air. Although we had both acted immaturely in certain ways, we handled the discord in the right way. We sat down with our wives to hash it out. I told Jeff how he had acted arrogantly at different times and had hurt my feelings. He, in turn, shared with me how I had belittled him with cutting remarks numerous times. We both acknowledged our fault in the matter and repented to each other. Then the four of us got on our knees, held hands and—with tears streaming down our cheeks—repented to the Lord over our actions.

Nothing ever came between the four of us again after that incident. A deep sense of trust was established because we made ourselves vulnerable to each other on that level. This, in turn, created an environment of trust for everyone on staff at the ministry. Walls that had been erected over minor disagreements began to come down.

It had been nearly seven years since Kathy and I first visited the Faith Homes. The deeper life teachings we received there—along with the writings of men like Andrew Murray, Charles Spurgeon, Watchman Nee, A.W. Tozer, Oswald Chambers, and others—had now permeated every aspect of the ministry. The Lord established a high biblical standard of living at Pure Life. Every employee was expected to live a consecrated life—separated from the foul influences of the world. Each was also required to spend at least two hours in personal devotions in the morning. In addition to all of that, we all had to do our utmost to live in a spirit of mercy and compassion to each other and to those sent to us by the Lord. God was requiring an all-out commitment from every member of the staff.

George Mooney discovered this not long after he became a staff member. One of the issues that remained buried in his heart was that now that he was on staff, he could take it easy. He had paid the price. He had gone through the live-in program. He had made it through the intern program. Therefore, he could now enjoy the benefits of being on staff and assumed he could handle the job by relying on his natural abilities with people. He really didn't need to press into God. To put it simply, George entered a phase of spiritual laziness. This time, the Lord used Rose Colón to help him see where he was spiritually.

One morning, in the staff prayer time, she confessed "what a witch" she could be inside at times. As humble and kind as Rose is, nobody else would ever think of her in that way. Nevertheless, she knew what was in her heart, and she did not mind confessing it in front of others. A few days later, she spoke in a Thursday evening worship service. She was in the fire of God and everybody was affected.

In the meantime, I was feeling a growing sense of conviction that George was backsliding in his heart. A few days later, he spoke in a Sunday evening meeting. Everybody enjoys him because he is adorable by nature, but I did not feel the presence of the Lord when he spoke. His words were dead and lifeless.

The next morning, I felt led to talk with him. "George, how are you doing spiritually?" I asked.

"Good, everything is going fine!" he replied confidently.

"George, when Rose describes her spiritual condition, she calls herself a witch. And yet when she gets up to speak to the men in the meeting, the presence of God fills the place. But when I ask how you are doing, everything is great, and yet when you speak in the meeting, your words are nothing but a lot of hot air!" I challenged.

It was easy to see the difference between the two. Rose was living in a sense of her unworthiness before

We really didn't realize it at the time, but the presence of God was gradually increasing at Pure Life.

a holy God. George, on the other hand, was full of self-confidence. In his prideful condition, he simply did not feel a great need for God's help in his daily life. This confrontation was just what he needed to get himself back on track. From then on, George began to take his walk seriously again.

Unquestionably, the Lord has been very strong with every PLM staff member. He has established something very precious to Him at this ministry and has no intention of allowing it to slip away due to apathy. We really didn't realize it at the time, but the presence of God was gradually increasing at Pure Life until it often became similar to the way it had been at the Faith Homes. Nowhere is this truer than during those times when the Holy Spirit takes over our meetings.

We try to run our services somewhat loosely rather than overly control them to the point that God cannot do something different than what we had planned. This open-ended approach allows staff members to stand up between songs during the worship time and share what they sense the Lord is putting on their hearts. In countless meetings through the years, the Lord has established a theme during the service that perfectly paves the way for the coming sermon. Many times one of the staff has read the exact verse that the preacher was going to exposit in his message. It is so marvelous to allow the Holy Spirit to direct the meetings, as opposed to having a canned service controlled by man from beginning to end.

Two recent services show how the Lord can take charge

when allowed. One Sunday morning, I felt led to open the meeting by sharing the fact that God is constantly speaking and that we need to listen to hear His words. I went on to talk about how the Lord makes the written Word come alive in a person's heart through the inward work of the Holy Spirit. Unbeknownst to me, Jeff—who was preaching that morning—had already prepared a sermon about the Word of God. When he got up to speak, the way had already been prepared.

Another instance occurred during our worship service the following Thursday evening. Earlier that day, the staff spent a half-day in corporate prayer. Every ministry leader felt a growing sobriety in their spirits throughout the four-hour period. So in the service, God's presence was manifested very powerfully. When He draws near in that way, one becomes much more attuned to the spiritual realm. God had been dealing very strongly with Justin that day, and he finally stood up in the meeting, with tears streaming down his cheeks, and repented to the Lord. He said, "Lord, I hear You calling. I'm coming, Lord. I'm coming!"

After he sat down, we sat in silence for a few minutes. Then I felt a word from the Lord rising up from within. I tried to hold it back, but finally blurted out, "There are people in this room who God has called to His feast, but you keep stalling. Your opportunities to respond to Him are running out!" Several people immediately dropped to their knees right where they were sitting and began repenting. We sat in silence again for a few minutes, and then I felt a strong sense that we should sing a *Vineyard* song entitled, "Who Will Ascend?" Jeff is our worship leader, and I

Visitors are often taken by surprise by the strong sense of the Lord's nearness in our worship times.

know he prays over the choice of songs before each service. I hated to disrupt his selection but leaned over to him and asked if we could sing that song. He responded, "Steve, that *is* the next song." This is typical of the way the Holy Spirit controls our meetings.

Visitors are often taken by surprise by the strong sense of the Lord's nearness in our worship times. One such visitor was Charlie Hungerford, a magazine editor who came to check out the ministry. He wrote the following as an editorial for his publication:

> While working on (an) issue of *HonorBound* Magazine, I had the distinct privilege to visit Pure Life Ministries. As I turned off the narrow black-topped road into the ministry's property, I felt a physical peace descend on me. It wasn't the location; this particular intersection of latitude and longitude is no more a part of God's creation than any other location. It is the very fact that these few acres are bathed in prayer and filled with men who are willing to admit their failures and follow hard after God...
>
> I didn't really go to Pure Life Ministries with any expectations. What I experienced, however, changed my entire perspective of what it means to submit to God's authority in my life. Young men, middle-aged men, men who had been pastors, men just like me, all together in one place for one reason. They had come to a point in life where they acknowledged a need for God to do a work in their lives... To the men at Pure Life, you have my respect. Your seriousness at following hard after God is an encouragement to me.
>
> One of the reasons people feel the presence of

God so strongly at Pure Life is the long hours the staff spends seeking the Lord. This is done during private devotions as well as a corporate time of prayer and Bible study Monday through Friday. We also get together once a month for either a half or full day of prayer. We emphasize prayer so much because we believe only God has the power to transform a man's heart. A man who has been bound up in something as powerful as pornography and sexual addiction desperately needs an encounter with the Living God. For the most part this prayer life is accomplished in our daily lives.

On one occasion we decided to spend an entire day seeking the Lord for a deeper infilling of the Holy Spirit. Anticipation built up during the days leading up to it. We didn't know what to expect. On the one hand, I wanted to encourage everybody to believe God to do something marvelous in our midst. However, I was also concerned that we would get our hopes too high and set ourselves up for a real disappointment.

We culminated a three-day fast during the day of prayer. That morning was spent worshipping the Lord, meditating on Scripture, and praying both silently and corporately. I started getting a little concerned when no "tongues of fire" had settled on the chapel roof by mid-afternoon, so I called Doug to get his feedback. He and Millie already knew about what we were doing and had been praying for us. "Steve," he said, "I have the sense that God is going to do something, but it isn't going to be exactly what you're expecting. The other thing I felt this morning when I was praying for you was that this is primarily going to be an unfolding of something inside all of you in the days to come. You are not nec-

essarily going to see anything visible today."

I appreciated Doug's
sensitivity to the Lord.
There are no words to ex-

*Suddenly the entire chapel
was filled with an atmosphere
of overflowing love.*

press what it has meant to be able to turn to him and Millie
over the years when we needed advice or prayer. However,
I must admit I was a little disappointed as I returned to the
chapel. I informed the others of what he said, and we all sat
in silence for a moment. I frankly didn't know what to do.
As we were sitting there, I walked up to the platform to
grab some cough drops. As I passed Jeff on the way back to
my seat, a surge of love for him rose up in my heart. I hugged
him and told him that I loved him. Then I noticed Rose
sitting there and I felt love for her; so I did the same with
her. Suddenly the entire chapel was filled with an atmosphere of overflowing love. Everybody stood up spontane-
ously and began hugging each other. This was not the gush-
ing sentimentalism of emotional people but a real outpour-
ing of the Holy Spirit. When it was all over, we could testify
along with the apostle Paul who said, "...the love of God
has been poured out within our hearts through the Holy
Spirit who was given to us." (Romans 5:5)

The love and devotion the staff has for each other
filters down to the men. In one sense, it creates the same
kind of security a child feels when he sees his mommy
and daddy openly expressing their love for each other. At
Pure Life, we have been very open about our devotion to
each other and to the men. This, in turn, helps them learn
to love others. Many of these men have never known
that kind of love in their entire lives. They don't need
dry sermons about God's love. They need to experience
it through His people.

There has been much growth at Pure Life since the early days of the ministry. My speaking schedule has intensified as I have spent many weekends ministering in churches and men's conferences across the country. Many doors have also opened for me to speak throughout Latin America. The live-in program—which began with six troubled souls—now accommodates 50 men. The staff presently consists of twenty people but continues to grow as hungry people long to be a part of what God is doing here. We have also had to purchase new properties to make room for all of the increase.

However, building up this organization was not the "new thing" that the Lord predicted in December 1996. The fulfillment of that prophecy has been to strengthen and fortify the foundation of this ministry. For one thing, the Lord has given the leadership much greater insight into the spiritual lives of those to whom we minister. Not only has He inspired me to write a number of books dealing with important Christian subjects from a "deeper life" perspective, but He has also given our counseling staff a wonderful gift of discernment. There has also been an increase in the flow of God's love through the lives of the employees. God's presence on the property and in the meetings has also intensified over the years. Without these elements, the work going on at Pure Life Ministries would tend to be superficial and ineffective at best.

In 2002, we hosted our first annual *Purity & Intimacy Conference.* This was not a seminar about sexual addiction but rather a continuation of the day of prayer we have had amongst the staff for several years. The tears of joy flowed freely as God's presence fell in a powerful way. At the end of the first conference, Doug came to me to express his gratitude. "Steve," he said earnestly, "this is just like it was in the Faith Homes!" That was the highest tribute to this ministry that I could ever hear.

Pure Life Ministries has become a well for other thirsty souls to drink from the living waters of Jesus Christ!

Ten years prior to this— back in 1992—Kathy, Lance and myself had pleaded with God for the abundant life evident in the Scriptures. As an answer to that cry, He led us to the Faith Homes where we were taught how to possess real Christianity and how to give it away to others. God has marvelously answered our prayers! Pure Life Ministries has become a well for other thirsty souls to drink from the living waters of Jesus Christ!

Out of the depths I have cried to Thee, O LORD...

I sought the LORD, and He answered me, and delivered me from all my fears. This poor man cried and the LORD heard him, and saved him out of all his troubles. O taste and see that the LORD is good; how blessed is the man who takes refuge in Him!

Who is the man who desires life, and loves length of days that he may see good? The eyes of the LORD are toward the righteous, and His ears are open to their cry. The righteous cry and the LORD hears, and delivers them out of all their troubles. The LORD is near to the brokenhearted, and saves those who are crushed in spirit. Many are the afflictions of the righteous; but the LORD delivers him out of them all. (Psalm 130:1; 34:1-4, 6, 8, 12, 15, 17-19)

Kathy Gallagher

Epilogue

I can honestly say that when I married Steve Gallagher twenty-four years ago, I never thought I'd end up with the man he is today. In fact, when I think back on what Steve was like in those early years, I am amazed at what the Lord has done, how He has taken the wretch Steve was and transformed him into a loving, humble man of God.

As is typical of Steve, he has openly shared some of his most embarrassing failures, his deepest secrets, and his greatest struggles in this book. He has willingly exposed that side of his life so that others facing similar struggles might find hope as they read these stories. But what Steve has shied away from, and what I am here to do, is to share with you how wonderfully different a man he is today, having been lifted out of the mire by the mighty hand of God. "You are the only one who knows the whole story," he told me. "You know what God has done in my life better than anybody else."

The road my husband took from darkness to light has been anything but smooth sailing. There has never been a time in his tumultuous past that he coasted; he simply did not have the luxury to do so. Steve also gave up any illusions about his ability to change himself early on. Having proved time and again that he didn't have what it took to get the kind of victory he needed, he did the only thing he knew to do: he laid hold of God until he received the answers he so desperately yearned for. In fact, I don't think I have ever seen a person more relentless to find God than my husband.

Steve has persistently allowed God to put him through the refiner's fire so that his heart's impurities might be burned away. And, while it has been very hot at times, he continues to subject himself to the Lord's chastisement. As a result, he has experienced a depth of repentance I have seen in very few people.

As a husband, Steve has far exceeded any dreams I ever had. I am hesitant to say much about something that is so precious to me. I don't want to cheapen it by using worn out phrases such as, "He is good to me," "He loves me," and so on. Those things are true, but his love for me is so much deeper than those little phrases could ever convey. Humanly speaking he is the best friend I have ever known. He tells me the truth about his struggles, letting me all the way into his heart and mind. He treats me with kindness, gently reproves me when I am out of line, and encourages me when I am afraid. There are times he tells me how pretty I am, but I know that it's not that I am pretty but that his heart has been filled with God's love for me. Steve has faithfully led me to Jesus for many years now, always insisting that the Lord be first in my heart and life. He has been Jesus to me in many ways.

The great transformation he has undergone is not limited to our home, however. He has become a gentle and loving man who deeply cares for other people. He is the complete opposite of everything he used to be. There have been times that I have been amazed to watch him patiently work with a scoffer or rebel. Rather than dealing with people according to his old methods, Steve usually handles such situations in the same way Jesus would: he tells them the truth in such a way that they feel loved and corrected at the same time!

As a leader, the degree of loyalty he receives from his staff is a marvelous testimony to the kind of man he is. Each of his staff knows that Steve has spent many hours praying them through their battles and failures. His concern for them isn't cheapened by flattery but is proven by his passion to see them find everything they need in God alone.

Each of them knows he is more concerned about how they are doing spiritually than he is with their work. He refuses to "use" people or promote someone simply because they have the ability to do a job well. Because the spiritual climate of Pure Life is too precious to him, compromise, on a ministry or personal level, is not an option. His primary agenda as the leader of this ministry is to shepherd his staff and ensure their spiritual well-being, even at the cost of ministry expansion or recognition. He continues to blaze a spiritual trail for others to follow, going before us and leading by example.

This leads me to his most distinguishing quality as a man: his love and pursuit of God. For the past nineteen years, I have watched him get up at 4 or 5 a.m. every morning to meet with his Lord. Whether at home or on the road, this remains a constant in his life. I suppose in the end, the worth of a man in God's Kingdom is not measured by how many people he preached to or how many books he wrote, but by the love he has for God and others. Steve Gallagher lives his life to know God, and the story of what the Lord has done (and continues to do) in his life can be an inspiration to any who see their need to change.

And what about you, dear reader? Has Steve's testimony stirred up a hunger to know God in a more meaningful way? Has the Lord attempted to deal with you about areas in your life that He isn't pleased with? Have you been faithful to pursue God with a passion? Are you living out His love to those people He has brought across your path?

These are important questions to consider. If the Lord has used this book to call you to Himself in a greater way, please be careful not to hurry on to the next "thing." Now might be one of the best opportunities you will have to examine your life and seek the Lord for the kind of transformation you have read in my husband's story. I trust that as you do so, you too will find that God can also do a marvelous work in your life—just as He did in the life of Steve Gallagher!

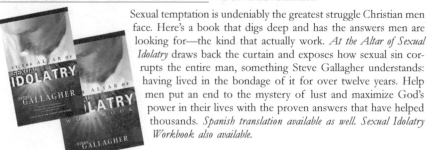

LIVING IN VICTORY

The secret to victorious living is to tap into God's great storehouse of mercy for one's own needs, and then act as a conduit for that power, directing it toward the lives of others. Overcoming habitual sin is important, but real victory occurs when a person becomes a weapon in the hands of a powerful God against the legions of hell. That is Living in Victory!"
—Steve Gallagher

BREAK FREE FROM THE LUSTS OF THIS WORLD

Break Free From the Lusts of This World is by far Steve Gallagher's best writing; its strength is his sobering deliverance of the unvarnished truth to a Church rife with sensuality and worldly compromise. In a time when evangelical Christians seem content to be lulled to sleep by the spirit of Antichrist, *Break Free From the Lusts of This World* sounds a clarion wake-up call in an effort to draw the Body of Christ back to the Cross and holy living. Those with itching ears will find no solace here, but sincere believers will experience deep repentance and a fresh encounter with the Living God.

THE WALK OF REPENTANCE

The Walk of Repentance is a 24-week Bible study for any Christian that desires to be more deeply consecrated to God. Each week of this easy-to-use curriculum has a theme, addressing the everyday challenges believers face one step at a time. Its simplicity is its strength, using only the Word of God—and occasional stories of saints of old—as its content. Experience the times of spiritual refreshing that follow repentance; go deeper in God as you allow His Word to take root in your heart.

VIDEOS

BREAKING FREE FROM HABITUAL SIN

People try all kinds of methods to break sinful habits, but God has only given one answer to habitual sin: Repentance. Find the freedom you seek; allow the Lord to tear down your old way of thinking and loose the chains that bind you.

OVERCOMING INSECURITY

Insecurities… how many of us have felt their paralyzing effects; yet, how few of us recognize them as the blight of pride? Allow the Lord to dismantle those crippling defense mechanisms that keep you from the abundant Christian life.

WHEN THE TEMPLE IS DEFILED

Christian men in sexual sin often need a wake-up call, a message that pins them to the floor in repentance. This sermon, filmed at Zion Bible Institute during a day of prayer and fasting, describes what happens to those who desecrate their inner being with pornography and sexual sin. God's presence was very strong and used this message to spark great repentance.

AUDIO

BREAKING FREE FROM THE POWER OF LUST— *OUR MOST POPULAR SERIES!*

The insidious beast of lust can entrap a person to the point of hopeless despair, but the Lord has given answers that work! The biblical revelations imparted in this series will break the power of lust in the believer's heart. (Four Tapes)

Pure Life Ministries

Pure Life Ministries helps Christian men achieve lasting freedom from sexual sin. The Apostle Paul said, "Walk in the Spirit and you will not fulfill the lust of the flesh." Since 1986, Pure Life Ministries (PLM) has been discipling men into the holiness and purity of heart that come from a Spirit-controlled life. At the root, illicit sexual behavior is sin and must be treated with spiritual remedies. Our counseling programs and teaching materials are rooted in the biblical principles that, when applied to the believer's daily life, will lead him out of bondage and into freedom in Christ.

Biblical Teaching Materials

Pure Life offers a full line of books, audiotapes and videotapes specifically designed to give men the tools they need to live in sexual purity.

Residential Care

The most intense and involved counseling the staff offers comes through the **Live-in Program** (6-12 months), conducted on the PLM campus in Kentucky. The godly and sober atmosphere at Pure Life Ministries provokes the hunger for God and deep repentance that destroys the hold of sin in men's lives.

Help At Home

The **Overcomers At Home Program** (OCAH) is available for those who cannot come to Kentucky for the live-in program. This twelve-week counseling program features weekly counseling sessions and many of the same teachings offered in the Live-in Program.

Care For Wives

Pure Life Ministries also offers help to wives of men in sexual sin. Our wives' counselors have suffered through the trials and storms of such a discovery and can offer a devastated wife a sympathetic ear and the biblical solutions that worked in their lives.

Pure Life Ministries
P.O. Box 410
Dry Ridge, KY 41035
(859) 824-4444—Office
(888) 293-8714—Order Line
info@purelifeministries.org
www.purelifeministries.org